Landauer Books

Quilts for Wilderness Kids

by Debbie Field
for Granola Girl™ Designs©

Copyright© 2002 by Landauer Corporation

Projects Copyright© 2002 by Debbie Field

This book was designed, produced, and published by Landauer Books
A division of Landauer Corporation
12251 Maffitt Road, Cumming, Iowa 50061

President/Publisher: Jeramy Lanigan Landauer
Vice President Sales & Marketing: James L. Knapp
Vice President Editorial: Becky Johnston
Creative Director: Laurel Albright
Project Editor: M. Peg Smith
Editorial Coordinator: Kimberly O'Brien
Technical Illustrator: Barb Gordon
Graphic Artist: Ann Shuman
Production Artist: Pat Seifert
Photographer: Craig Anderson Photography

ISBN: 1-890621-32-3
This book is printed on acid-free paper.
Printed in USA

10 9 8 7 6 5 4 3 2

Willow Furniture available from

Windy Ridge Flowers & Willow Furniture
1269 Fig Avenue
Coon Rapids, IA 50058
712-684-5285

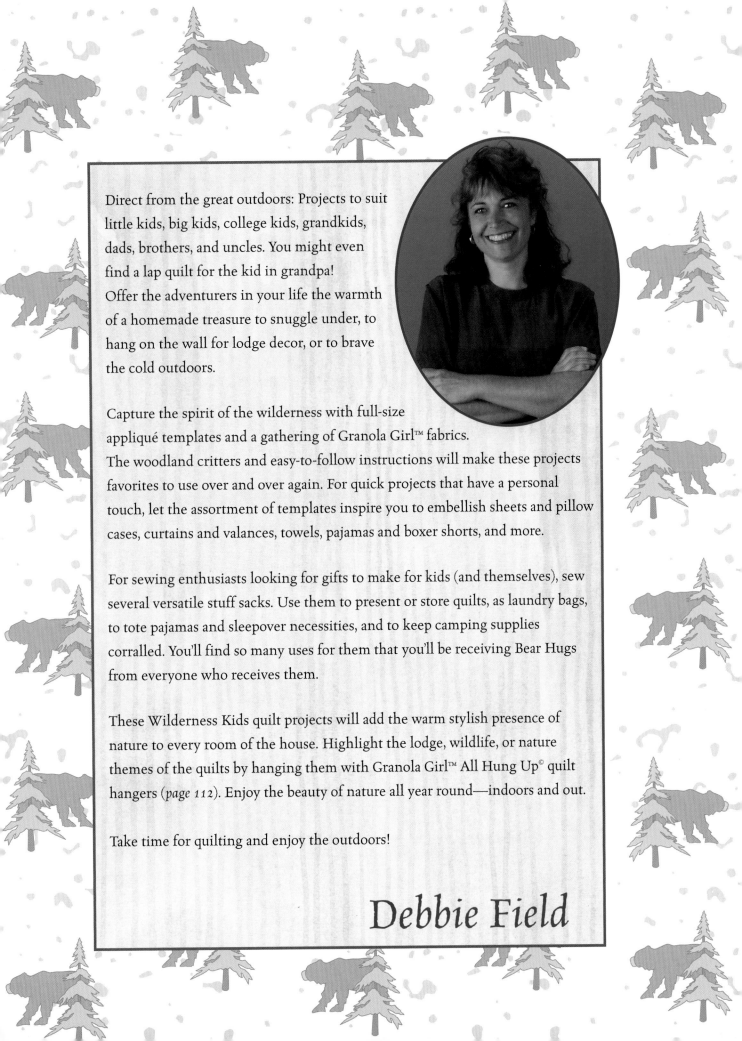

Direct from the great outdoors: Projects to suit little kids, big kids, college kids, grandkids, dads, brothers, and uncles. You might even find a lap quilt for the kid in grandpa! Offer the adventurers in your life the warmth of a homemade treasure to snuggle under, to hang on the wall for lodge decor, or to brave the cold outdoors.

Capture the spirit of the wilderness with full-size appliqué templates and a gathering of Granola Girl™ fabrics. The woodland critters and easy-to-follow instructions will make these projects favorites to use over and over again. For quick projects that have a personal touch, let the assortment of templates inspire you to embellish sheets and pillow cases, curtains and valances, towels, pajamas and boxer shorts, and more.

For sewing enthusiasts looking for gifts to make for kids (and themselves), sew several versatile stuff sacks. Use them to present or store quilts, as laundry bags, to tote pajamas and sleepover necessities, and to keep camping supplies corralled. You'll find so many uses for them that you'll be receiving Bear Hugs from everyone who receives them.

These Wilderness Kids quilt projects will add the warm stylish presence of nature to every room of the house. Highlight the lodge, wildlife, or nature themes of the quilts by hanging them with Granola Girl™ All Hung Up© quilt hangers (*page 112*). Enjoy the beauty of nature all year round—indoors and out.

Take time for quilting and enjoy the outdoors!

Debbie Field

About
the Artist

Debbie Field, producing her work
through Granola Girl™ Designs,
has emphasized her love of the
outdoors in quilts, wallhangings,
books, patterns, accessories,
and her own fabric lines.
Her work is a reflection of personal
experiences since childhood—
with the breathtaking sights
of nature and wildlife of the great
northern woods.

She attributes her outdoor spirit to
the warmth of her family and living an
adventurous outdoor lifestyle—
a tradition instilled by her parents that
continues with her husband and
her sons and their families.

Contents

General Instructions

Assemble the tools and supplies to complete the project. In addition to basic cutting and sewing tools, the following will make cutting and sewing easier: small sharp scissors to cut appliqué shapes, rotary cutter and mat, extra rotary blades, and a transparent ruler with markings.

Replace the sewing machine needle each time you start a project to maintain even stitches and to prevent skipped stitches and broken needles during the project. Clean the machine after every project to remove lint and to keep it running smoothly.

The projects shown are made with unwashed fabrics. If you prewash fabrics, purchase extra yardage to allow for shrinkage. The 100-percent cottons and flannels used in the wilderness quilts and accessories are from Debbie's Granola Girl™ collection: Nature's Way, Nature's Tracks, Making Tracks, Legends, and Winter Memories. These fabrics are manufactured by Troy Corporation—ask for them where you shop for fabrics.

Please read through the project instructions before cutting and sewing. Square the fabric before cutting and square it again after cutting 3 or 4 strips. Align the ruler accurately to diagonally cut squares into triangles. Sew with 1/4" seam allowances throughout, unless stated otherwise in the instructions, and check seam allowance accuracy to prevent compounding even slight errors. Press seams toward the darker fabric when possible. When pressing small joined pieces, press in the direction that creates less bulk.

Basic Appliqué

Please note that the printed appliqué templates are reversed. Trace and cut the templates as printed, unless the illustrations and photos indicate to reverse the templates. For appliqués that face the opposite direction, trace and reverse the template. Dashed lines indicate design overlap.

Trace the appliqué template to the fusible webbing with a fine tip marker or sharp pencil, allowing space to cut 1/4" beyond the traced lines. Position the fusible web on the wrong side of the appliqué fabric. Follow the webbing manufacturer's instructions to fuse the webbing to the fabric. Allow the fabric to cool and cut along the traced line. Remove the paper backing and follow the pattern placement to position the appliqué pieces on the background fabrics.

Use lightweight tear-away stabilizer to machine appliqué. Place the stabilizer beneath the fabric layers and use a small, tight zigzag stitch to sew around each shape, smoothly covering the raw fabric edge. If your machine has stitch options, use them to detail appliqués—such as fishing lines, animal eyes and noses, fish fins and scales, etc. After the stitching is complete, remove the stabilizer according to the manufacturer's instructions.

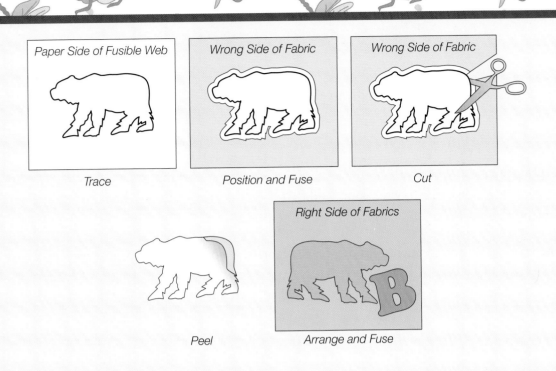

Trace — Paper Side of Fusible Web

Position and Fuse — Wrong Side of Fabric

Cut — Wrong Side of Fabric

Peel

Arrange and Fuse — Right Side of Fabrics

Basic **Binding**

Join binding strips for a continuous length. Fold the strip in half lengthwise, right sides out, and press. Match the raw edges of the folded strip to the quilt top, along a lower edge and approximately 6" form a corner, allowing approximately 6" free to join to the opposite end of the binding. Avoid placing binding seams on corners. Sew the binding to the quilt top with a 1/4" seam allowance (see Step 1).

At the first corner, stop 1/4" from the corner, backstitch, raise the presser foot and needle, and rotate the quilt 90 degrees. Fold the binding back onto itself to create a miter (see Step 2), then fold it along the adjacent seam (see Step 3), matching raw edges. Continue sewing to the next corner and repeat the mitered corner process. Where the binding ends meet, fold under one binding edge 1/4", encase the opposite binding edge, and stitch it to the quilt top.

Trim the batting and backing fabric even with the quilt top and binding. Fold the binding strip to the back of the quilt and handsew it in place with a blind stitch. Sign and date the quilt, including the recipient's name if it is a gift.

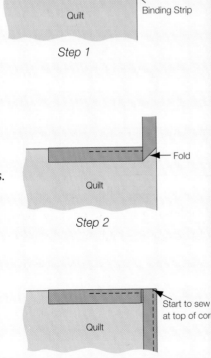

Step 1 — Quilt, Binding Strip

Step 2 — Quilt, Fold

Step 3 — Quilt, Start to sew at top of corner

Welcome to Bear Country

Bear Hugs

Quilt

Finished size is approximately 57x73".

Materials

Light flannel fabric
1-1/4 yards for blocks

Dark (rust) flannel fabric
1 yard for blocks

Medium fabric
1 yard for sashing and inner border

Medium-light fabric
2-2/3 yards
for
outer border
and binding

Bear Hugs *appliqué templates on pages 62–64,
and the following assorted fabrics:*

Black woodgrain-print flannel—
5/8 yard for #1, #4, #11, and foot and paw claws
Brown-fleck flannel—
5/8 yard for #2 #5, #9, #12, and #15
Black-fleck flannel—
5/8 yard for #3, #6, #8, #10, #13, and #14
Gray—scrap for #7 (inside eye pupil)

Fusible web—3-1/2 yards

Stabilizer

Sulky® Thread to match fabrics

Batting—63×79"

Backing fabric—3-3/4 yards

Cut the Fabrics

From Light:

- Cut 2—7-5/8" strips; cut strips into 6—7-5/8" squares; cut each square diagonally for 12 half-square triangles.

- Cut 3—4-1/4" strips; cut strips into 24—4-1/4" squares; cut each square diagonally for 48 half-square triangles.

- Cut 2—3-7/8" strips; cut strips into 12—3-7/8" squares.

From Dark:

- Cut 2—7-5/8" strips; cut strips into 6—7-5/8" squares; cut squares diagonally for 12 half-square triangles.

- Cut 3—4-1/4" strips; cut strips into 24—4-1/4" squares; cut each square diagonally for 48 half-square triangles.

From Medium:

- Cut 11—2-1/2" strips. Cut 2 strips into 8—2-1/2x10-1/2" rectangles. Use 9 strips for the sashing and inner border.

From Medium-light:

- Cut 1—12-1/2" strip for the top of the outer border.

- Cut 5—9-1/2" strips for the sides and bottom of the outer border.

- Cut 7—3" binding strips.

Note: Cut and fuse the appliqué pieces, following the General Instructions on *pages 6–7.*

11

Assembly

1. Right sides facing, join one light and one dark 4-1/2" half-square triangle. Press each seam toward the dark fabric. Repeat to sew 48 triangle squares for Unit A.

Unit A

2. Join two Unit A triangle squares, as shown *below,* to make 12 Unit B rectangles. Press each seam toward the dark fabric.

Unit B

3. Note triangle placement and join 24 triangle squares, as shown *below,* to make 12 Unit C rectangles. Press each seam toward the dark fabric.

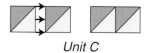

Unit C

4. Join the 3-7/8" light squares to Unit C for 12 of Unit D. Press each seam toward the square.

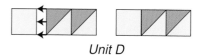

Unit D

5. Join 7-5/8" half-square triangles for 12 Unit E triangle squares. Press seams toward dark fabric.

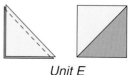

Unit E

6. Join Units B and E, noting placement, to make 12 of Unit F. Press seams toward the large triangle.

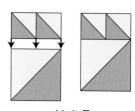

Unit F

7. Sew Unit D to the left side of Unit F, noting placement, to make 12 Bear Paws blocks. Press the seams toward Unit D.

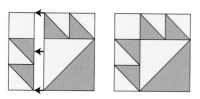

8. Sew the 2-1/2x10-1/2" medium rectangles to the blocks, as shown *below,* to make 4 rows of 3 blocks. Press the seams toward the sashing.

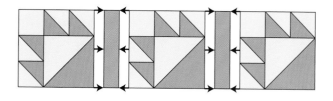

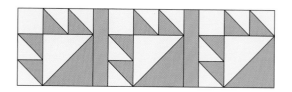

9. Measure the row width through the center for sashing length. Cut 5—2-1/2" sashing strips to that length. Join the rows with sashing and sew a sashing strip to the bottom and top of the rows.

10. Measure the lengthwise center of the quilt for the side sashing strips. Cut 2 strips to that length and sew them to the sides. Press seams toward the sashing.

11. Measure through the center width of the quilt top for top and bottom border lengths. Cut one 12-1/2" and one 9-1/2" strip to length. Sew the 12-1/2" strip to the top and the 9-1/2" strip to the bottom of the quilt. Press the seams toward the borders.

12. Measure through the center length of the quilt top and cut 2 outer border strips to that length. Sew the borders to the quilt top and press the seams toward the borders.

13. Refer to the illustration, *below,* for placement and General Instructions, *pages 6–7,* to cut, fuse, stabilize, and appliqué the pattern pieces.

14. Layer backing, batting, and the quilt top. Baste the layers and hand- or machine-quilt as desired. Finish the quilt by sewing on the binding, following the steps in the General Instructions, *pages 6–7.*

Finished Quilt Assembly

13

Bear Hugs

Pillow

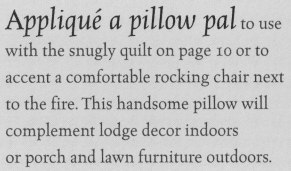

Appliqué a pillow pal to use with the snugly quilt on page 10 or to accent a comfortable rocking chair next to the fire. This handsome pillow will complement lodge decor indoors or porch and lawn furniture outdoors.

Finished size approximately 34" square.

Materials

Light fabric
22" square for background

Medium fabric
1/3 yard for inner border

Dark fabric
1-1/2 yard for outer border and backing

Bear Hugs *appliqué templates on page 62, and the following assorted fabrics:*

Black—
1/2 yard for #1, #3, #6, and #10

Darkest brown—
1/2 yard for #2, #9, and #11

Dark brown—
5x10" for #4

Brown—
10" square for #5, #8, and #12

Gray—scrap for #7 (inside eye pupil)

Fusible web—2-1/2 yards

Stabilizer

Black and brown Sulky® Thread

Batting—1 yard square

Muslin—1 yard square

Pillow form—34" square

Assembly

1. Fuse bear head pieces #1—#12 onto background fabric. Refer to the General Instructions on *pages 6–7* to fuse, stabilize, and appliqué the fabrics. Use matching thread and a small zigzag stitch around each shape.

2. For the inner border, cut 2—2×22" and 2—2×25"strips. Sew the 22" strips to the sides of the pillow top; press the seams toward the borders. Sew the 25" strips to the top and bottom of the pillow top; press the seams toward the borders.

3. For the outer border, cut 2—4-3/4×25" strips. Sew them to the sides; press the seams toward the borders. Cut 2—4-3/4×33-1/2" strips and sew them to the top and bottom. Press the seams toward the borders.

4. Layer the pillow top, batting, and muslin; quilt as desired. Trim the batting and muslin.

5. Right sides of pillow top and backing fabric facing, stitch 1/4" around the pillow top, allowing an opening to turn to the right side.

6. Insert a pillow form or fiberfill. Slip-stitch the opening closed.

Pillow Top Assembly

Bear Country

Quilt

Finished size approximately 49x65".
Each Anvil Block is 16" square.

Materials

Light fabric
1-1/4 yards for background

Medium-print fabric
1/3 yard for block center

Dark fabric
1/3 yard for half-square triangles

Rust-print fabric
1/2 yard for inner border

Medium Blue bear-print fabric
2 yards for outer border and binding

Bear Country *appliqué templates on pages 65–67,
and the following assorted fabrics:*

Black—1/2 yard for bear

Medium brown—scrap for nose

Green—1/2 total of 3 shades for trees

Brown—1/4 yard for tree trunks

Fusible web—1-1/2 yards

Stabilizer

Sulky® Thread to match fabric

Batting—55x71"

Backing fabric—3 yards

These ambling bears invite

you to take a walk through the woods.
Rich, dark colors and tree appliqués that
extend beyond the borders of the forest
create warm texture for a full-size throw
or a small bed cover.

Cut the Fabrics

From Medium:
- Cut 1—8-1/2" strip; cut the strip into
  4—8-1/2" squares for the block center.

From Dark:
- Cut 2—4-7/8" strips; cut the strips into
  16—4-7/8" squares. Diagonally cut each
  square for 32 half-square triangles.

From Light:
- Cut 2—8-1/2x32-1/2" rectangles.

- Cut 2—4-7/8" strips. Cut each strip into
  16—4-7/8" squares. Diagonally cut each
  square for 32 half-square triangles.

- Cut 2—4-1/2" strips. Cut each strip into
  16—4-1/2" squares.

From Rust-print:
- Cut 5—2-1/2" inner border strips.

From Medium Blue bear-print:
- Cut 6—6-1/2" outer border strips.

- Cut 6—3" binding strips.

Note: Cut and fuse the appliqué
pieces, following the General
Instructions on *pages 6–7.*

17

Assembly

1. Right sides facing, join one dark and one light half-square triangle. Press the seam toward the dark fabric. Repeat to sew 32 triangle squares for Unit A.

Unit A

2. Referring to the illustration, *below,* for placement, join a Unit A to a Unit A for 8 of Unit B and 8 of Unit C. Press seams toward the dark triangle.

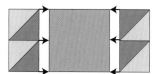

Unit B   *Unit C*

3. Sew a Unit B to the left and right side of the four 8-1/2" squares, noting placement direction. Press the seams toward the square.

4. Sew two light 4-1/2" squares to each Unit C. Press the seams toward the squares.

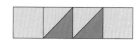

5. Sew the units to the top and bottom of each block. Press seams toward the block center.

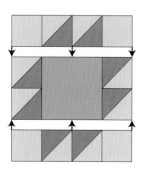

6. Sew the Anvil blocks together as shown in the diagram, *below.* Sew the 8-1/2×32-1/2" rectangles to the top and bottom. Press the seams toward the rectangles.

7. Sew together 3 inner border strips for a continuous length. Measure the quilt through the center and cut 2 strips to that length. Sew the strips to the quilt top sides and press the seams toward the border.

8. Measure the quilt width through the center, cut 2 strips to that length. Sew the strips to the top and bottom, and press the seams toward the border.

9. Join the outer border strips. Cut 2 strips the length of the quilt top and sew them to the sides of the quilt. Press the seams toward the border.

10. Measure and cut 2 strips to the quilt top width and sew them to the top and bottom. Press the seams toward the outer border.

11. For the bear appliqué templates, trace 1 large bear and 2 reversed; trace 2 small bears and 2 reversed. For the trees, trace 11 of #1, 13 of #2, 6 of #3, and 5 of #4. Trace 5 small and 6 large tree trunks. Refer to the illustration, *opposite,* for placement and to the General Instructions, *pages 6–7,* to position and fuse, and appliqué pieces.

12. Layer the quilt backing fabric, batting, and quilt top. Baste the layers together; hand- or machine-quilt as desired. Finish the quilt by sewing on the binding, following the steps in the General Instructions, *pages 6–7.*

Finished Quilt Assembly

Wilderness Camping

Camping in the Woods

Quilt

Finished size approximately 49x54".

Materials

Light fabric
2-1/8 yards for background

Medium Green fabric
1 yard for Flying Geese (trees)

Dark fabric
3/8 yard for tree trunks

Medium Blue fabric
1/2 yard for inner border

Dark-print fabric
1-3/4 yards for outer border and binding

Camping in the Woods *appliqué templates on pages 68–75,* **Bear Country** *large bear appliqué on page 66, and the following assorted fabrics:*

Brown—10x12" for moose body

Black—7x10" for bear

Orange/dark yellow—4x5" for fire

Tan—10x14" for tent

Off-white—9x10" for inside of tent, eagle head and tail, and raccoon mask

Gray—3 each for raccoon, 2 wolves, and stones

Green—3 each for brush/bushes

Brown—6 for moose antlers, bear nose, squirrel, eagles, deer, tent pole, squirrel tree limb, and fire logs

Fusible Web—2-3/4 yards

Stabilizer

Sulky® Thread to match fabrics

Batting—55x60"

Backing fabric—2-1/2 yards

All *the* delightful creatures

of the forest have assembled in this peaceful setting. Let this snuggler quilt or wallhanging inspire story-telling of favorite camping adventures— real and imaginary!

Cut the Fabrics

From Light:
- Cut 8—5-1/2" strips; cut each strip into
  40—5-1/2" squares and
  2—5-1/2x10-1/2" rectangles.

- Cut 4—4" strips; cut each strip into
  4—4x20-1/2" rectangles and
  4—4x15-1/2" rectangles.

From Medium Green:
- Cut 3—10-1/2" strips; cut each strip into
  20—5-1/2x10-1/2" rectangles.

From Dark:
- Cut 2—3-1/2" strips; cut each strip into
  2—3-1/2x15-1/2" strips and
  2—3-1/2x20-1/2" strips.

From Medium Blue:
- Cut 5—2-1/2" strips for the inner border.

From Dark-print:
- Cut 6—5-1/2" strips for the outer border.

- Cut 6—3" strips for binding.

Note: Refer to illustrations for number of templates to trace and cut. Cut and fuse, following the General Instructions on *pages 6–7.*

Assembly

1. Lay a light 5-1/2" square on the right side of a green 5-1/2x10-1/2" rectangle. Draw a diagonal line along the center of the square. Sew along the line and trim the seam allowance of the square to 1/4". Press the triangle toward the green fabric.

2. Lay a square on the left side of the rectangle, draw a line, sew, trim the seam and press. Repeat to make 20 Flying Geese units.

3. Sew together two strips of 6 Flying Geese units, as shown *below*. Press seams up on one strip and down on the other.

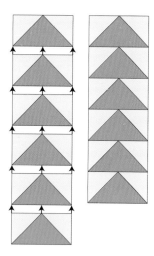

4. Sew together two strips of 4 Flying Geese units; sew a 5-1/2x10-1/2" rectangle to the top of each unit. Press the seams up on one strip and down on the other.

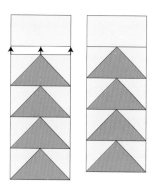

5. Sew two light 4x15-1/2" strips and two light 4x20-1/2" strips to each long side of a dark trunk strip, matching lengths, to make 4 tree trunks. Press the seams toward the dark fabric.

2 - 10-1/2x15-/2" Units   2 - 10-1/2x20-1/2" Units

6. Join short tree trunk units to 6-part Flying Geese units. Join long tree trunk units to 4-part Flying Geese units. Press the tree units.

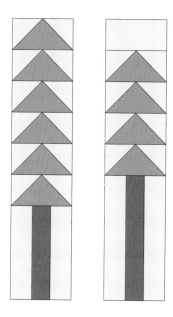

7. Join the tree units, as shown *below*, and press.

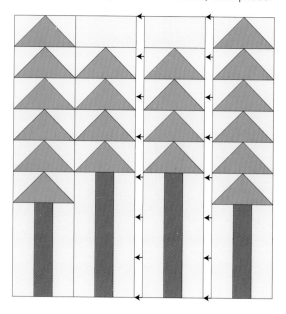

8. Measure the quilt top through the center width. Cut 2 strips that length and sew to the top and bottom. Press the seams toward the border.

9. Measure the quilt top lengthwise through the center for the side borders. Cut 2 strips to length and sew to the sides. Press seams toward the border.

10. Following Steps 8 and 9, sew the outer border to the quilt top.

11. Refer to the illustration, *below,* and the pattern pieces for appliqué placement. Sew around the fabric pieces with small zigzag stitches.

12. Layer the backing, batting, and quilt top. Baste the layers together, and quilt by hand or machine as desired. Finish the quilt by sewing on the binding, following the steps in the General Instructions, *pages 6–7.*

Finished Quilt Assembly

Lonely Moose

Wallhanging

*Finished size approximately 43" square.
Each Anvil Block is 16" square.*

Materials

Medium print fabric
1/3 yard for block center

Dark-print fabric
1/3 yard for half-square triangles

Light fabric
2/3 yard for background

Medium fabric
1/2 yard for inner border

Dark fabric
1-1/4 yards for outer border and binding

Lonely Moose *appliqué templates
on pages 76–77,*
Bear Country *tree templates on pages 65 and 67,
and the following assorted fabrics:*

Dark brown—5x6" for moose head,
1-1/2x9" for large tree trunk

Brown—7" square for moose body

Woodgrain-print fabric—4" square for antlers

Green—6x8" for tree (#1–#3)

Blue—4x12" for water

Fusible Web—1/2 yard

Stabilizer

Sulky® Thread to match fabrics

Batting—48" square

Backing fabric—1-1/2 yards

Capture the spirit of the wilderness with the regal independence of a singular moose. Bold Anvil Blocks frame the moose and his natural setting to create a wallhanging that is equally suited to the den, family room, or hallway.

Cut the fabric

From Medium-print:
- Cut 1—8-1/2" strip; cut the strip into 4—8-1/2" squares.

From Dark-print:
- Cut 2—4-7/8" strips; cut the strips into 16—4-7/8" squares. Diagonally cut each square into 32 half-square triangles.

From Light:
- Cut 2—4-7/8" strips; cut each strip into 16—4-7/8" squares. Diagonally cut each square into 32 half-square triangles.
- Cut 2—4-1/2" strips; cut each strip into 16—4-1/2" squares.

From Medium:
- Cut 4—1-1/2" strips for the inner border.

From Dark:
- Cut 4—5" strips for the outer border.
- Cut 5—3" strips for binding.

Note: Cut and fuse the appliqué pieces, following the General Instructions on *pages 6–7.*

Assembly

1. Right sides facing, join one light and one dark print half-square triangle. Press the seam toward the dark fabric. Repeat to sew 32 triangle squares for Unit A.

Unit A

2. Referring to the illustration, *below,* for placement, join a Unit A to a Unit A for 8 of Unit B and 8 of Unit C. Press seams toward the dark triangle.

Unit B   *Unit C*

3. Sew a Unit B to the left and right side of the four 8-1/2" squares, noting placement, *below*. Press the seams toward the squares.

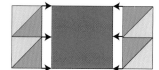

4. Sew two light 4-1/2" squares to each Unit C. Press the seams toward the end squares.

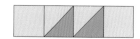

5. Sew the units to the top and bottom of the block. Press seams toward the center square.

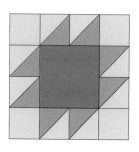

6. Join the Anvil Blocks, as shown in the Finished Wallhanging Assembly, *opposite.*

7. Measure the quilt through the center length. Cut 2—1-1/2" inner border strips to length. Sew each to a side of the quilt, and press the seams toward the border.

8. Measure the quilt width through the center and cut the remaining 1-1/2" strips to length. Sew the strips to the top and bottom and press the seams toward the border.

9. For the outer border, measure the quilt length and cut 2—5"strips to length. Sew the borders to the quilt sides and press the seams toward the border.

10. Measure the quilt width, cut the remaining outer borders to length, sew them to the top and bottom, and press the seams toward the border.

11. Refer to the appliqué placement, *opposite,* and the General Instructions, *pages 6–7,* to fuse and place appliqué pieces to the blocks. Use small zigzag stitches around each shape.

12. Layer the backing fabric, batting, and quilt top. Baste the layers together and quilt the wallhanging by hand or machine as desired. Finish the quilt by sewing on the binding, following the steps in the General Instructions, *pages 6–7.*

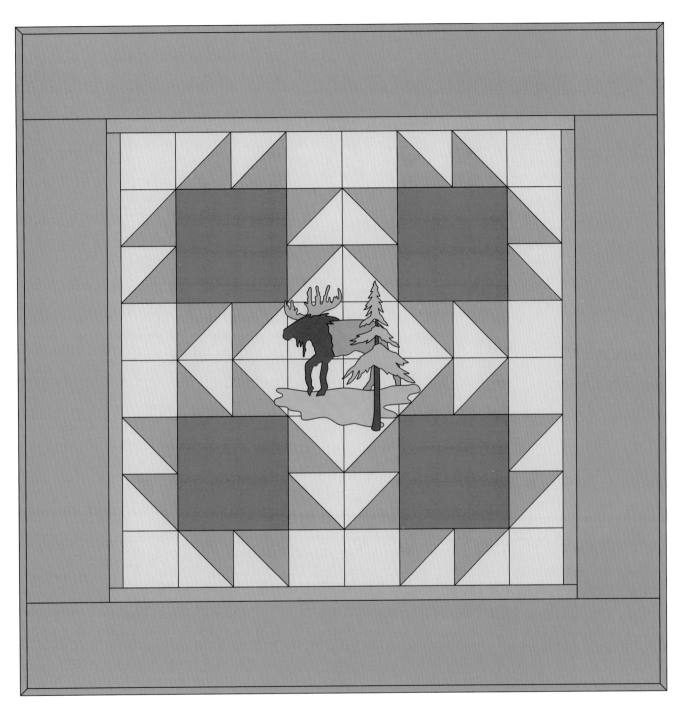

Finished Wallhanging Assembly

Wolf Pack

Quilt

Wolves howling is a familiar sound on a moonlit night in the dark forest. In this quilt, you can appreciate the silent and graceful beauty of the creatures, using dark fabrics for wolves and blocks and bright gold for a moon.

Finished size approximately 49x65".
Anvil Blocks are16" squares.

Materials

Medium print fabric
1/3 yard for block center

Black fabric
1/3 yard for half-square triangles

Light print fabric
1-1/4 yards for background

Medium Blue print fabric
1/2 yard for inner border

Rust/black leaf print fabric
2 yards for outer border and binding

Wolf Pack appliqué templates on page 78, **Bear Country** tree templates #1–4 on pages 65 and 67, and the following assorted fabrics:

Grayish brown—1/2 yard for wolves

Light green—1/3 yard for 1 large and 5 small trees

Dark green—1/4 yard for 1 small and 3 large trees

Dark brown—1/4 yard for tree trunks

Gold—4" square for moon

Fusible web—2-1/2 yards

Stabilizer

Sulky® Thread to match fabrics

Batting—55x70"

Backing fabric—3 yards

Cut the Fabrics

From Medium print:
- Cut 1—8-1/2" strip; cut the strip into 4—8-1/2" squares.

From Black:
- Cut 2—4-7/8" strips; cut each strip into 16—4-7/8" squares. Diagonally cut each square for 32 half-square triangles.

From Light print:
- Cut 2—8-1/2x32-1/2" rectangles.
- Cut 2—4-7/8" strips; cut each strip into 16—4-7/8" squares. Diagonally cut each square for 32 half-square triangles.
- Cut 2—4-1/2" strips; cut each strip into 16—4-1/2" squares.

From Medium Blue print:
- Cut 5—2-1/2" strips.

From Rust on black leaf print:
- Cut 6—6-1/2" strips.
- Cut 6—3" strips.

Note: Cut and fuse the appliqué pieces, following the General Instructions on *pages 6–7.*

Assembly

1. Right sides facing, join one light and one dark half-square triangle. Press the seam toward the dark fabric. Repeat to sew 32 triangle squares for Unit A.

Unit A

2. Referring to the illustration, *below,* for placement, join a Unit A to a Unit A for 8 of Unit B and 8 of Unit C. Press seams toward the dark triangle.

Unit B   *Unit C*

3. Sew a Unit B to the left and right side of the four 8-1/2" squares, noting placement, *below*. Press the seams toward the squares.

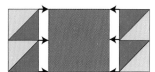 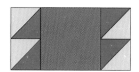

4. Sew two light 4-1/2" squares to each Unit C. Press the seams toward the squares.

5. Sew the unit to the top and bottom of the block. Press seams toward the block center.

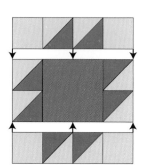 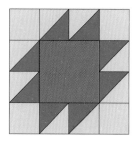

6. Join the Anvil Blocks as shown *below.* Sew the 8-1/2x32-1/2" rectangles to the top and bottom. Press the seams toward the rectangles.

7. Join 3 inner border strips for a continuous length. Measure the quilt length through the center; cut 2 strips to that length. Sew the strips to each side of the quilt top. Press the seams toward the border.

8. Measure the quilt width through the center and cut the remaining 2 strips to that length. Sew the strips to the top and bottom of the quilt. Press the seams toward the border.

9. Join the outer border strips. Cut 2 strips the length of the quilt top and sew them to the sides of the quilt. Press seams toward the border.

10. Measure and cut 2 strips to the quilt top width and sew them to the top and bottom. Press the seams toward the outer border.

11. For the wolf template, trace 3 and 2 reversed. For the tree templates, trace 9 of #1, 9 of #2, 8 of #3, and 3 of #4. Trace 4 large and 5 small tree trunks. Refer to appliqué placement, *opposite,* and General Instructions, *pages 6–7,* to fuse, position, and appliqué pieces to the quilt blocks.

12. Layer backing fabric, batting, and quilt top. Baste the layers together. Quilt by hand or machine. Sew on the binding following the steps in the General Instructions, *pages 6–7.*

32

Finished Quilt Assembly

Finished pillow top is approximately 19" square.

Materials for one Pillow

Light fabric
8-1/2" square for block center

Dark fabric
1/4 yard for half-square triangles

Medium fabric
1/3 yard for background

Coordinating fabric
1 yard for border and backing

Fusible web

Stabilizer

Sulky® Thread to match fabrics

18" pillow form or 1 bag of fiberfill

For the **Eagle** Pillow,
use **Eagle Ridge** appliqué template on *page 92*,
Bear Country tree templates on *pages 65 and 67*,
and the following assorted fabrics:

Brown—for tree trunk and eagle body

Green—for tree

Tan—for eagle beak

White/Off-white—for eagle head and tail

For the **Tree Line** Pillow,
use **Bear Country** tree appliqué templates
(3 #1, 3 #2, 3 #3, 1 #4) on *pages 65 and 67*,
and the following assorted fabrics:

Brown—for tree trunks

Green—for trees

For the **Wolf** Pillow,
use **Wolf Pack** appliqué template (reversed)
on *page 78*, and the following fabric:

Brown—for wolf

Complement North Woods

or Lodge decor with a plush assortment of wilderness designs. Highlight a singular theme or combine your favorites to create plump, comfortable pillows for kids of all ages.

Cut the fabric

From Light:
- *Cut 1—8-1/2" square.*

From Dark:
- Cut 1—4-7/8" strip; cut the strip into 4—4-7/8" squares. Diagonally cut each square into 8 half-square triangles.

From Medium:
- Cut 1—4-7/8" strip; cut the strip into 4—4-7/8" squares. Diagonally cut each square into 8 half-square triangles.
- Cut 1—4-1/2" strip; cut the strip into 4—4-1/2" squares.

From Coordinating fabric:
- Cut 2—2x16-1/2" strips.
- Cut 2—2x19-12" strips.

Note: Cut and fuse the appliqué pieces, following the General Instructions on *pages 6–7.*

Assembly

1. Right sides facing, join one dark and one light half-square triangle. Press the seam toward the dark fabric. Repeat to sew 8 triangle squares for Unit A.

Unit A

2. Referring to the illustration, *below,* for placement, join a Unit A to a Unit A for 2 of Unit B and 2 of Unit C. Press seams toward the dark triangle.

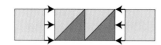

Unit B   *Unit C*

3. Sew a Unit B to the left and right side of the 8-1/2" square, noting placement direction. Press the seams toward the square.

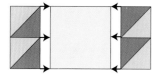

4. Sew two light 4-1/2" squares to each Unit C. Press the seams toward the squares.

5. Sew the unit to the top and bottom of the block. Press seams toward the block center.

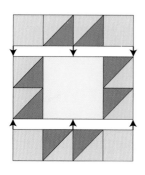

6. Sew a 2×16-1/2" strip to each side of the block. Press the seams toward the border.

7. Sew the 2×19-1/2" strips to the top and bottom of the block. Press the seams toward the border.

8. Refer to the appliqué placement, *opposite,* and the General Instructions, *pages 6–7,* to fuse and position the appliqué pieces to the quilt block. Use a small zigzag stitch and matching thread around each shape to appliqué it to the block.

9. Right sides facing, layer the pillow top and backing. Stitch around the outer edge, leaving an opening for turning and inserting a pillow form or fiberfill.

10. Turn the pillow top to the right side. Insert the form or fiberfill, and slip-stitch the opening closed.

Finished Pillow Top Assembly

Stuff

Sacks

Finished size approximately 21x33".

Materials for one Stuff Sack

Fabric—1 yard for sack

Cording—2 yards

Fusible web—1/2 yard

Sulky® Thread

Busy Beaver Stuff Sack *appliqué templates on pages 78–79, and the following assorted fabrics:*

Brown—for beaver body and branches

Dark brown—for tail

Black—for face

Ecru—for tooth

Light/Medium Brown—for feet

Green—for leaves

Wood-grain fabric—for tree stump

Camping in the Woods *appliqué templates on pages 68–69, 71–72, and 74, and the following assorted fabrics:*

Gold plaid—for the tent

Ecru—for inside the tent

Brown—in 2 shades for logs and tent pole

Orange/yellow—for fire

Gray—for stones

Wolf Pack *appliqué templates (reversed) on page 78,* **Bear Country** *tree templates on pages 65 and 67, and the following assorted fabrics:*

Gray—for wolf

Green—for trees

Gold—for moon

Woodgrain-print fabric—for tree trunks

Bear Country *large bear appliqué templates on page 66 and the following assorted fabrics:*

Black—for bear

Light brown—for nose

Green—for trees

Wood-grain fabric—for tree trunks

Stuff sacks are welcomed

carryalls to tote sleeping bags, snuggle quilts, pajamas and sleepover essentials, laundry, and all the necessary gear that kids tend to stash and carry. Because the sacks go together quickly and you can individualize each sack with favorite wilderness appliqué designs, you'll want to make several for all the wildlife enthusiasts on your gift list.

Assembly

1. Square the 1-yard fabric piece.
2. Fold the fabric in half, wrong sides facing, referring to the illustration *below.* Trim off the selvage edges.

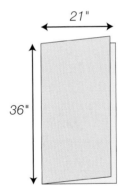

21"

36"

Assembly continued

3. With the fabric folded, measure 8" from the lower raw edge. Mark the point with a pin to serve as a guide for appliqué placement.

4. Referring to the General Instructions on *pages 6–7,* fuse the appliqué pieces.

5. Refer to the illustrations, *opposite,* for design placement. Center the fused pieces on the sack panel, aligning them with the placement mark. Use a small, tight zigzag stitch around the appliqués in embroidery threads that match fabrics.

6. To finish the side edges of the sack, lay the fabric face down. Fold and press 1/4" along each long raw edge. Fold and press 1/4" again. Stitch through the center of the fold along each side using either a zigzag or straight stitch. (Or use a serger to finish the edges.)

Inside of sack

7. To make the drawstring casing, fold over and press 1/2" along the top raw edge. Fold over again by 2" and press. Stitch 1/4" from both folded edges to create a drawstring casing.

8. Finish the bottom edges by folding and pressing 1/4" along the bottom edge. Zigzag or straight stitch along the folded edge.

9. Right sides together and finished edges aligned, sew a 1/2" seam, stitching from the bottom folded edge, pivoting at the corner, stitching along the side, and backstitching at the casing edge. DO NOT SEW ACROSS THE CASING. To strengthen the seam, sew along the previous stitching line. Turn the sack right side out.

10. Knot or otherwise secure cording ends to prevent raveling. Secure a large safety pin in one end and thread the cording through the casing. Knot the cording ends together.

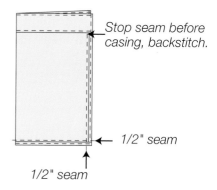

Stop seam before casing, backstitch.

1/2" seam

1/2" seam

Busy Beaver

Wolf Pack

Bear Country

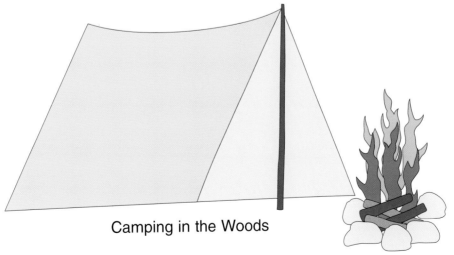

Camping in the Woods

Gone
Fishing
&
Hiking

Fishing Tales Quilt

*Finished size is approximately 49x65".
Each Anvil Block is 16" square.*

Materials

Medium blue fabric
1/3 yard for block center

Dark blue fabric
1/3 yard for half-square triangles

Light blue mottled fabric
1-1/4 yards for background

Medium green print fabric
1/2 yard for inner border

Medium blue marbled water print fabric
2 yards for outer border and binding

Fishing Tales *appliqué templates on pages 81–91
and the following assorted fabrics:*

Greens—1/3 yard each for oak leaves and cattail
rushes; small pieces for frog, water lily pads, turtle
shell, fish, sandbar island tree line, 3 shades for
Fish A, 2 shades each for Fish B, C, and D

Browns—1/3 for tree branch; small pieces for toad,
turtle, cattails and stems, canoe and
canoe trim, bare tree and sandbar island,
hair, man's pants, fishing pole, Fish B

Beige/tan—for faces and hands

Black—for fish and toad eyes

Blue—for water

Blue/Green—for shirts

Gray—2 shades for Fish D

Orange—for Fish B

Salmon speckled—for Fish C

White—for water ripple

Yellow—2 each for water lily buds

Fusible web—3-1/2 yards; Stabilizer

Sulky® Thread to match fabrics

Batting—55x70"; Backing—3 yards

Envision an early morning

outing—dad and son on a quiet lake,
sharing precious time and dreaming of
catching that big fish! These beautifully
detailed swimmers and shoreline critters
are cause for fishing reflections.

Cut the Fabric

From Medium blue:
- Cut 1—8-1/2" strip; cut the strip into
  4—8-1/2" squares.

From Dark blue:
- Cut 2—4-7/8" strips; cut each strip into
  16—4-7/8" squares. Diagonally cut each
  square for 32 half-square triangles.

From Light blue mottled:
- Cut 2—8-1/2x32-1/2" rectangles.
- Cut 2—4-7/8" strips; cut each strip into
  16—4-7/8" squares. Diagonally cut each
  square into 32 half-square triangles.
- Cut 2—4-1/2"strips; cut each strip into
  16—4-1/2" squares.

From Medium green print:
- Cut 5—2-1/2" strips for inner borders.

From Medium blue marbled water print:
- Cut 6—6-1/2" strips for outer borders.
- Cut 6—3" strips for binding.

Note: Cut and fuse the appliqué pieces,
following the General Instructions
on *pages 6–7.*

Assembly

1. Right sides facing, join one dark and one light half-square triangle. Press the seam toward the dark fabric. Repeat to sew 32 triangle squares for Unit A.

Unit A

2. Referring to the illustration, *below,* for placement, join a Unit A to a Unit A for 8 of Unit B and 8 of Unit C. Press seams toward the dark triangle.

Unit B   *Unit C*

3. Sew a Unit B to the left and right side of the four 8-1/2" squares, noting placement direction. Press the seams toward the squares.

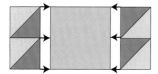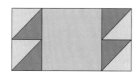

4. Sew two light 4-1/2" squares to each Unit C. Press the seams toward the squares.

5. Sew the unit to the top and bottom of the block. Press seams toward the block center.

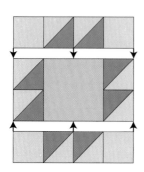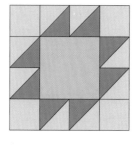

6. Join the Anvil Blocks as shown in the Finished Quilt assembly, *opposite.* Sew the 8-1/2x32-1/2" rectangles to the top and bottom of the block assembly. Press the seams toward the rectangles.

7. Join 3 inner border strips. Measure the quilt length through the center and cut 2 strips to that length. Sew the strips to each side of the quilt top and press the seams toward the border.

8. Measure the quilt width through the center and cut the remaining 2 strips to that length. Sew the strips to the top and bottom of the quilt, and press the seams toward the border.

9. Join the outer border strips. Cut 2 strips the length of the quilt top and sew them to the sides of the quilt. Press seams toward the border.

10. Measure and cut 2 strips to the quilt top width and sew them to the top and bottom. Press the seams toward the outer border.

11. Refer to the Finished Quilt Assembly, *opposite,* for placement and the General Instructions, *pages 6–7,* to fuse, position, and appliqué pieces to the quilt blocks. Use a small zigzag stitch and matching thread to appliqué around each shape.

12. Layer the quilt backing fabric, batting, and quilt top. Baste the layers together. Hand- or machine-quilt as desired. Finish the quilt by sewing on the binding, following the steps in the General Instructions, *pages 6–7.*

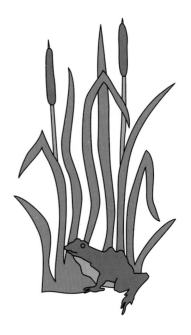

Finished Quilt Assembly

Eagle Ridge

Wallhanging

The majestic national

symbol of the United States of America soars among magnificent treetops. Your heart will leap at the beauty and tranquility of this textural depiction of nature's finest in flight.

Finished Wallhanging is approximately 43" square. Anvil Blocks are 16" square.

Materials

Medium sky-blue fabric
1/3 yard for the block center

Dark blue fabric
1/3 yard for half-square triangles

Light sky-blue fabric
2/3 yard for background

Dark blue with light print fabric
1/3 yard for inner borders

Medium blue print fabric
1-1/3 yards for outer border and binding

Eagle Ridge *appliqué templates on page 92,* **Bear Country** *Tree templates on pages 65 and 67, and the following assorted fabrics:*

Greens—3/8 yard total for trees

Dark Brown—for 2 eagles and 2 tree trunks

Medium Brown—for 2 eagles and 5 tree trunks

Gold—for eagle beaks

White—for eagle heads and tails

Fusible Web—1/2 yard

Stabilizer

Sulky® Thread to match fabrics

Backing—1-1/2 yards

Batting—49" square

Cut the Fabric

From Medium sky-blue:

- Cut 1—8-1/2" strip; cut the strip into 4—8-1/2" squares.

From Dark blue:

- Cut 2—4-7/8" strips; cut each strip into 16—4-7/8" squares. Diagonally cut each square for 32 half-square triangles.

From Light sky-blue:

- Cut 2—4-7/8" strips; cut each strip into 16—4-7/8" squares. Diagonally cut each square for 32 half-square triangles.

- Cut 2—4-1/2" strips; cut each strip into 16—4-1/2" squares.

From Dark blue with light print:

- Cut 4—1-1/2" strips for the inner borders.

From Medium blue print:

- Cut 4—5" strips for the outer borders.

- Cut 5—3" strips for the binding.

Note: Cut and fuse the appliqué pieces, following the General Instructions on *pages 6–7.*

Assembly

1. Right sides facing, join one dark and one light half-square triangle. Press the seam toward the dark fabric. Repeat to sew 32 triangle squares for Unit A.

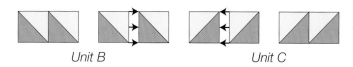

Unit A

2. Referring to the illustration, *below,* for placement, join a Unit A to a Unit A for 8 of Unit B and 8 of Unit C. Press seams toward the dark triangle.

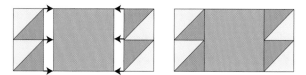

Unit B   *Unit C*

3. Sew a Unit B to the left and right side of the four 8-1/2" squares, noting placement direction. Press the seams toward the squares.

4. Sew two light 4-1/2" squares to each Unit C. Press the seams toward the squares.

5. Sew the unit to the top and bottom of the block. Press the seams toward the block center.

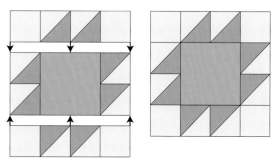

6. Join the Anvil Blocks as shown in the Finished Wallhanging Assembly, *opposite.*

7. Measure the quilt through the center length. Cut 2—1-1/2" inner border strips to length, sew them to each side of the wallhanging, and press the seams toward the border.

8. Measure the quilt width through the center and cut the remaining 1-1/2" strips to length. Sew the strips to the top and bottom and press the seams toward the border.

9. For the outer border, measure the quilt length and cut 2—5" strips to length. Sew the borders to the quilt sides and press the seams toward the border.

10. Measure the quilt width, cut the remaining outer borders to length, sew them to the top and bottom, and press the seams toward the border.

11. Trace 2 of the eagle template and 2 reversed. For the trees, trace 7 of #1, 7 of #2, 7 of #3, and 3 of #4. Refer to the Finished Wallhanging Assembly, *opposite,* for placement and the General Instructions, *pages 6–7,* to fuse, position, and appliqué pieces to the blocks. Use small, close zigzag stitches and matching threads to appliqué each shape.

12. Layer the backing fabric, batting, and quilt top. Baste the layers together and quilt the wallhanging by hand or machine as desired. Finish the quilt by sewing on the binding, following the steps in the General Instructions, *pages 6–7.*

50

Finished Wallhanging Assembly

Woodland ABCs

Quilt

Finished size approximately 56x68".
Pine Tree Blocks are 8×10".

Materials

Light print fabric—2 yards for background

Green fabric—1 yard for trees

Brown fabric—1/4 yard for tree trunks

Rust on navy leaf-print fabric—3/4 yard
for sashing and inner border

Rust small muted-print fabric—1-5/8 yard
for outer border and binding

Fusible web—3-1/2 yards

Stabilizer

Sulky® Thread to match fabrics

Backing—3-1/2 yards; Batting—62x74"

Woodland ABCs *templates on pages 93–103,*
Bear Country *small bear on page 65,*
Fishing Tales *turtle on page 81,*
and the following assorted fabrics:

Black—5x7" for bear body, 4x6" for loon; 3x6" for
skunk; small pieces for caterpillar belly, goose
neck; black-and-white multicolor for loon wing

Blue—water for fish, water for loon

Bright green—caterpillar body,

Brown—1/3 yard for alphabet, 5" square for moose
body, 3x9" for turtle body and head; small pieces
for bear nose, eagle beak and wings

Dark Brown—5" square for vole, 3x5" for otter,
4x5" for moose head, 4x8" for porcupine, 6x7" for
nest; small pieces for deer antlers, goose wing

Ecru or off-white—skunk back and tail,
eagle head and tail, raccoon mask

Gray-black print—6x7" for raccoon

Gray-brown—7x8" for wolf

Gray-blue print—nest eggs

Green—3x6" print for turtle shell; vole grass

Light Brown—4x6" for deer body, 6" square for vole
ground; small pieces for nest, goose body and
throat, otter chest and legs

Multicolor print—5x6" for fish

White—for deer chest, loon neck and chest,

Woodgrain-print—moose antlers

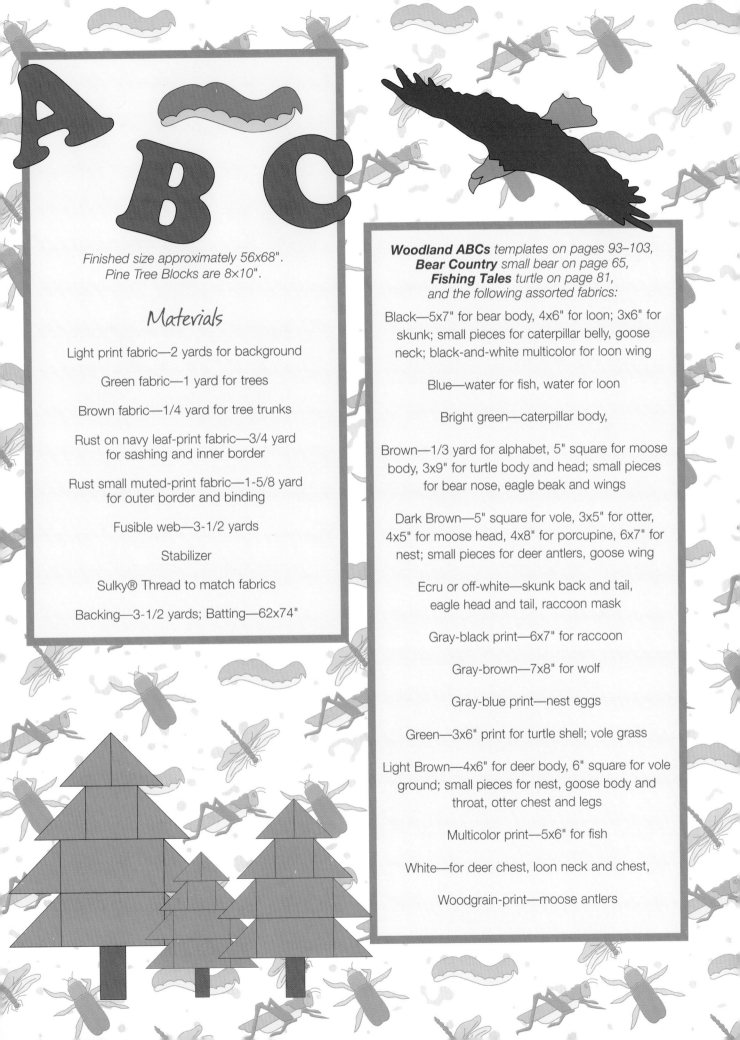

Cut the Fabric

From Light:

- Cut 3—10-1/2" strips; cut the strips into 10—10-1/2" squares and 2—8-1/2x10-1/2" rectangles for the appliqué blocks.

- Cut 2—2-7/8" strips; cut each strip into 26—2-7/8" squares. Diagonally cut each square for 52 Unit F half-square triangles.

- Cut 10—2-1/2"strips.

  Cut 4 strips into 26—2-1/2x4-1/2" Unit B rectangles.

  Cut 3 strips into 26—2-1/2x3-1/2" Unit E rectangles.

  Cut 3 strips into 26—2-1/2x4" Unit I rectangles.

From Green:

- Cut 2—2-7/8" strips; cut each strip into 26—2-7/8" squares. Diagonally cut each square for 52 Unit D half-square triangles.

- Cut 9—2-1/2" strips;

  Cut 1 strip into 13—2-1/2" Unit C squares.

  Cut 4 strips into 52—2-1/2" Unit A squares.

  Cut 4 strips into 26—2-1/2x4-1/2" Unit G rectangles.

From Brown:

- Cut 1— 2-1/2" strip; cut the strip into 13—1-1/2x2-1/2" Unit H rectangles.

From Rust on navy leaf-print:

- Cut 10—2-1/2" strips for sashing and inner border.

From Rust small muted-print:

- Cut 7—4-1/2" strips for the outer border.

- Cut 6—3" strips for binding.

  Note: Cut and fuse the appliqué pieces, following the General Instructions on *pages 6–7.*

Block Assembly

1. Mark a diagonal line along the wrong side of each of the 52 Unit A 2-1/2" green squares.

2. Using 26 Unit A squares and 26 Unit B rectangles, position Unit A facedown on Unit B, noting placement, *below.* Sew along the diagonal line to make 13 left units and 13 right units. Trim the seam to 1/4" and press each seam toward the dark fabric.

13 left units   *13 right units*

3. Join a left and right unit to make a tree top unit (Row 1, *below*) for 13 tree top units. Press the seams in the same direction.

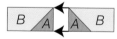  Row 1

4. Using 26 Unit A squares and 26 Unit E rectangles, place Unit A facedown on Unit E, noting placement, *below.* Sew along the diagonal line to make 13 left units and 13 right units. Trim the seam to 1/4" and press each seam toward the dark fabric.

13 left units   *13 right units*

5. Sew a left and right unit to opposite sides of Unit C to make Row 2, *below.* Press seams to the center.

  *Row 2*

6. Right sides facing, join a Unit D and Unit F half-square triangle to make 26 left and 26 right end units, *below.* Press seams toward the dark fabric.

    26 left   *26 right*
  end units   *end units*

7. Sew each left and right unit to opposite sides of a Unit G rectangle to make 26 units for Rows 3 and 4, *below.* Press the seams toward the center.

should read Rows (plural)

  *Row 3 and 4*

8. Sew a Unit I large rectangle to opposite sides of a Unit H small rectangle to make 13 Row 5 tree trunk units. Press the seams toward the center.

  *Row 5*

9. Layout and join Rows 1-5 to make 13 Pine Tree blocks. Press the seams toward the top of the tree. Set the blocks aside.

10. Layout, but DO NOT JOIN, the Pine Tree blocks and the Appliqué blocks, referring to the Finished Quilt Assembly on *page 56,* and using the 8-1/2x10-1/2" rectangles at the centers of Rows 2 and 4.

11. Refer to Finished Quilt Assembly, *page 56,* and General Instructions, *pages 6-7,* to fuse, position, and appliqué. Use a small zigzag stitch and matching thread. If the appliqué blocks distort from stitching, press and shape to size.

12. Sew the Pine Tree and completed Appliqué blocks together in 5 rows of 5 blocks each. The rows should measure approximately 44-1/2" wide.

13. Join the sashing and inner border strips for a continuous length. Measure the width of Row 1 through the center. Cut two lengths to that

measurement and sew one to each long edge of the row. Measure Rows 2, 3, 4, and 5; cut and sew a strip to the lower long edge *only* of each row. Join the rows and sashing strips. Press the seams toward the strips.

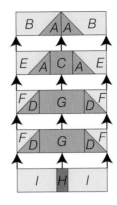 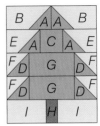

14. Measure the length of the quilt top through the center. Cut two inner border strips to that length and sew one to each side of the quilt. Press the seams toward the borders.

15. Join the outer border strips for a continuous length. Measure the length of the quilt top through the center. Cut two strips to that length and sew one to each side of the quilt top. Press the seams toward the borders. Measure the width of the quilt top through the center and cut two strips to that length. Sew one strip to the top and one strip to the bottom of the quilt. that length. Press the seams toward the borders.

16. Layer the backing fabric, batting, and quilt top. Baste the layers together and quilt by hand or machine as desired. Finish the quilt by sewing on the binding, following the steps in the General Instructions, *pages 6–7.*

Finished Quilt Assembly

Don't Bug Me

Quilt

Finished size approximately 44x65".
Nine-Patch and Rail Blocks measure 6" square.

Materials

Light solid fabric
1/2 yard for appliqué blocks and top panel

Light print fabric
3/4 yard for blocks

Dark green print fabric
1/3 yard for blocks

Medium green print fabric
2 yards for blocks,
outer border, and binding

Black background print
1/2 yard for sashing and inner borders

Don't Bug Me *appliqué templates
on pages 104–111
and the following assorted fabrics:*

Black—for caterpillar head, dragonfly, ants,
mosquito, beetle, eyes

Blue plaid—1/3 yard for letters

Brown—caterpillar, grasshopper,
dragonfly wings, beetle, mosquito

Brown/black—spiders

Green—praying mantis, grasshopper,
caterpillar, and millipede

Woodgrain-print—spiders, mosquito wings

Fusible web—1-3/4 yards

Stabilizer

Sulky® Thread to match fabrics

Backing fabric—3 yards

Batting—50x72"

For all those kids who like to keep bugs in a jar, here's the perfect solution! These bugs have no appetite for biting and there's no worry about breaking the jar. Just relax and inspect the fascinating colors and shapes.

Cut the Fabrics

From Light solid:
- Cut 1—8-1/2x30-1/2" strip.
- Cut 1—6-1/2" strip; cut the strip into
  6—6-1/2" squares.

From Light print:
- Cut 10—2-1/2" strips.

From Dark green:
- Cut 4—2-1/2" strips.

From Medium green:
- Cut 5—5-1/2" strips for the outer border.
- Cut 6—2-3/4" strips for binding.
- Cut 4—2-1/2" strips for blocks.

From Black background print:
- Cut 6—2" strips for sashing and
  inner border.

Assembly

1. Sew a dark green strip to each side of a light print strip. Repeat to make a second strip set. Press the seams toward the dark fabric. Cut the strip sets into 24—2-1/2x6-1/2" segments.

24—2-1/2x6-1/2"

2. Sew a light print strip to each side of a medium green strip. Repeat to make four strip sets. Press the seams toward the medium fabric. Cut the strips into 17—6-1/2" squares for Rail Blocks and 12—2-1/2x 6-1/2" segments that will be used to make Nine-Patch Blocks.

12—2-1/2x6-1/2"

12—2-1/2x6-1/2"
Rail Blocks

3. Assemble two dark-light-dark segments and one light-medium-light segment to make 12 Nine-Patch Blocks, shown *below*. Press the seams in one direction.

12—Nine Patch Blocks

4. Join the Nine-Patch Blocks with the Rail Blocks to form Rows 1, 3, 5, and 7, shown *below*. Press the seams toward the Rail Blocks. Join the

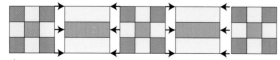

Rows 1, 3, 5, and 7

remaining Rail Blocks with the solid 6-1/2" squares to form Rows 2, 4, and 6, shown *below*. Press the seams toward the Rail Blocks.

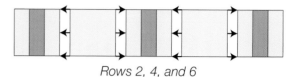

Rows 2, 4, and 6

5. Join the rows as shown in the Finished Quilt Assembly, *opposite.*

6. Refer to the Finished Quilt Assembly, *opposite,* for placement and the General Instructions, *pages 6–7,* to fuse, cut out, position, and appliqué the blocks and the 8-1/2x30" rectangle. Use a small zigzag stitch and matching or coordinating threads to appliqué each piece in place. *NOTE:* Dashed lines outside bug templates indicate stitching lines for details.

7. Sew a 30-1/2" sashing strip to the lower edge of the Don't Bug Me rectangle. Sew the joined piece to the block assembly. Press the seams toward the sashing strip.

8. Measure the quilt width along the center and cut two inner border strips to that length. Sew one strip to the top and one to the bottom of the quilt top. Measure the quilt top lengthwise through the center and cut two strips to that measurement. Sew one strip to each side of the quilt. Press the seams toward the borders.

9. Measure the quilt top widthwise through the center. Cut two outer border strips to length. Sew one to the top and one to the bottom of the quilt. Press the seams toward the borders. Measure the length of the quilt top, cut two outer border strips, and sew them to the sides of the quilt. Press seams toward the borders.

10. Layer the backing fabric, batting, and quilt top. Baste the layers together and quilt by hand or machine as desired. Finish the quilt by sewing on the binding, following the steps in the General Instructions on *pages 6–7.*

Finished Quilt Assembly

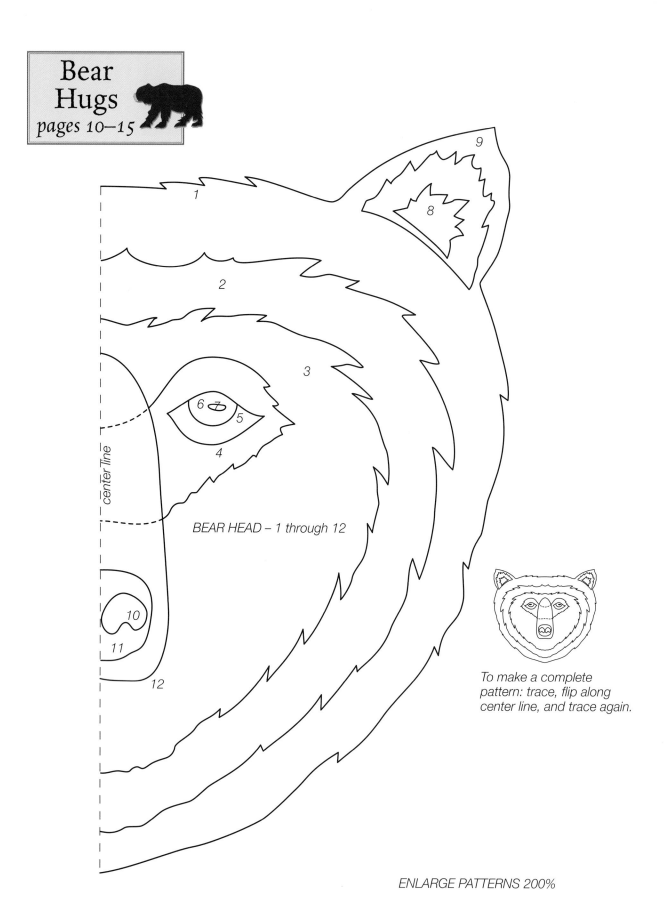

Bear Hugs

pages 10–15

1

2

3

6 7

5

4

center line

BEAR HEAD – 1 through 12

9

8

10

11

12

To make a complete pattern: trace, flip along center line, and trace again.

ENLARGE PATTERNS 200%

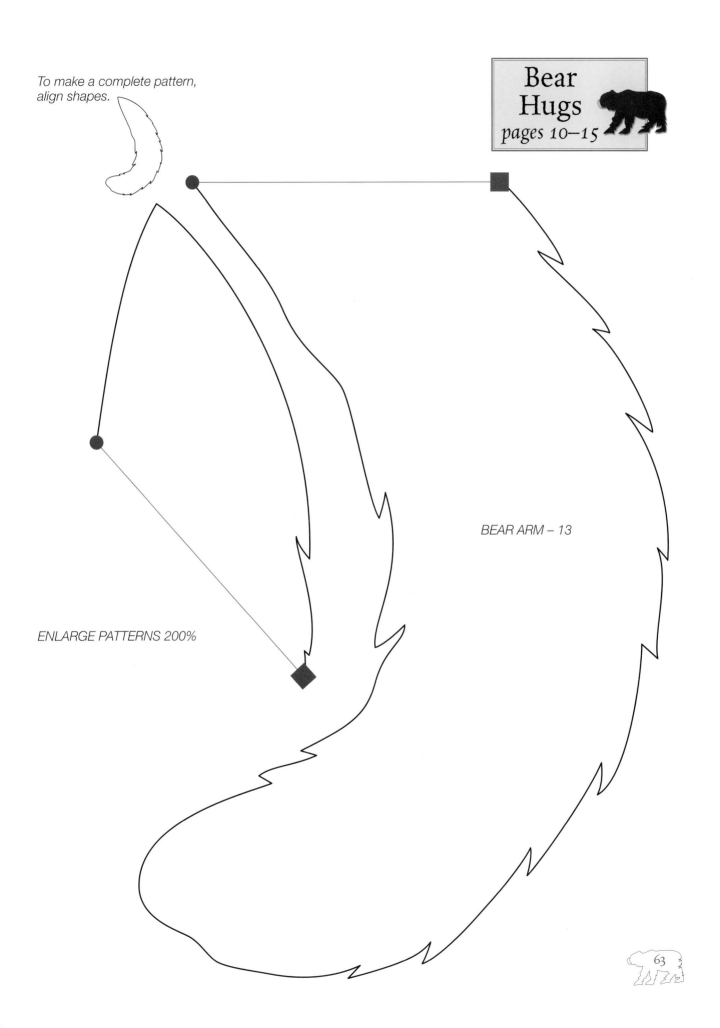

To make a complete pattern,
align shapes.

Bear
Hugs
pages 10–15

BEAR ARM – 13

ENLARGE PATTERNS 200%

63

Bear Hugs
pages 10–15

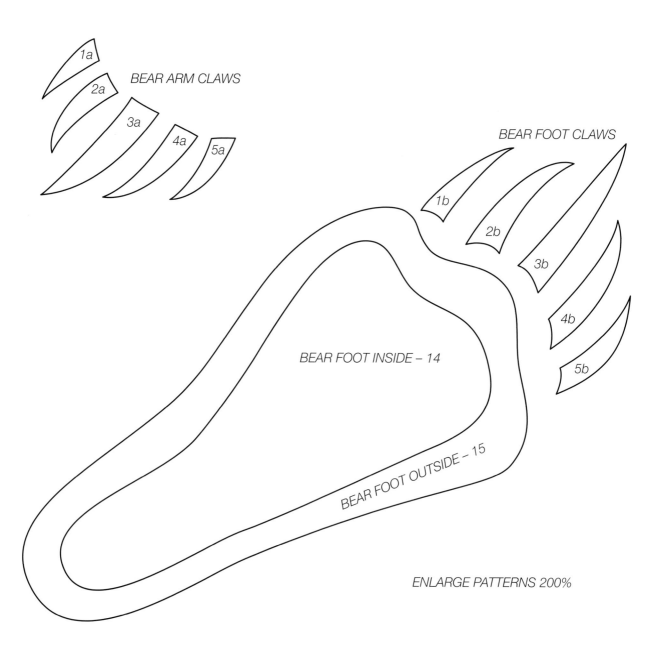

1a

BEAR ARM CLAWS

2a

3a

4a

5a

BEAR FOOT CLAWS

1b

2b

3b

4b

5b

BEAR FOOT INSIDE – 14

BEAR FOOT OUTSIDE – 15

ENLARGE PATTERNS 200%

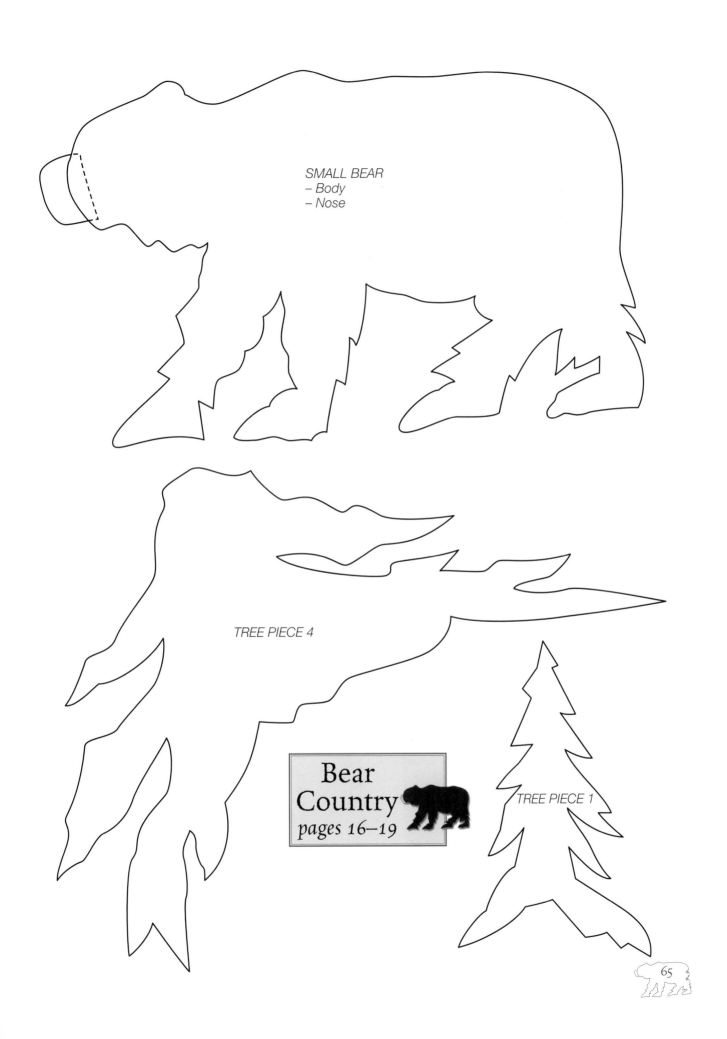

SMALL BEAR
– Body
– Nose

TREE PIECE 4

Bear
Country
pages 16–19

TREE PIECE 1

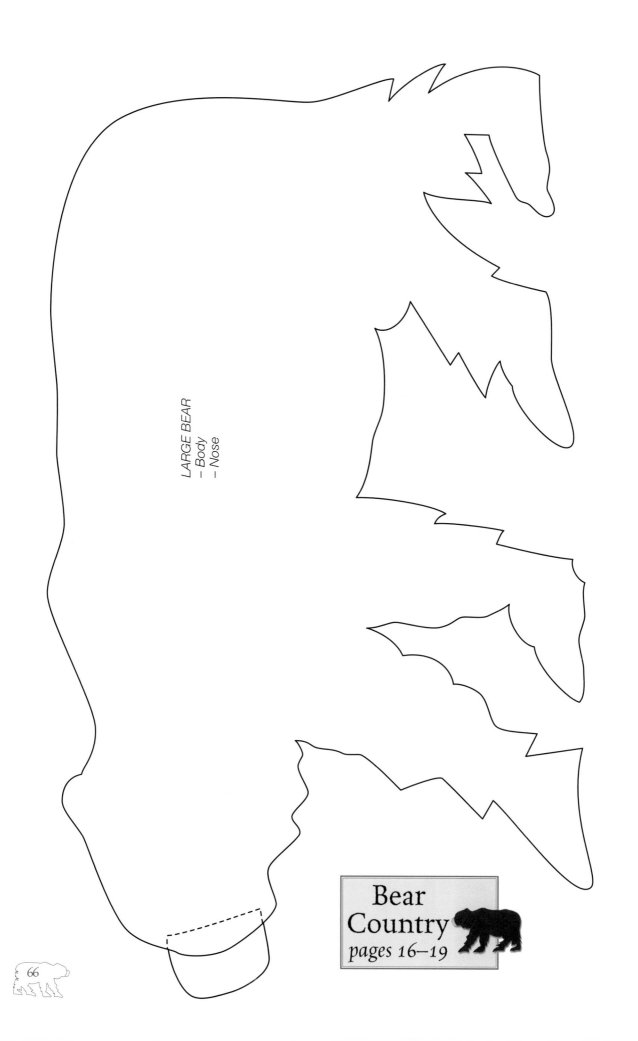

LARGE BEAR
- Body
- Nose

Bear
Country
pages 16–19

66

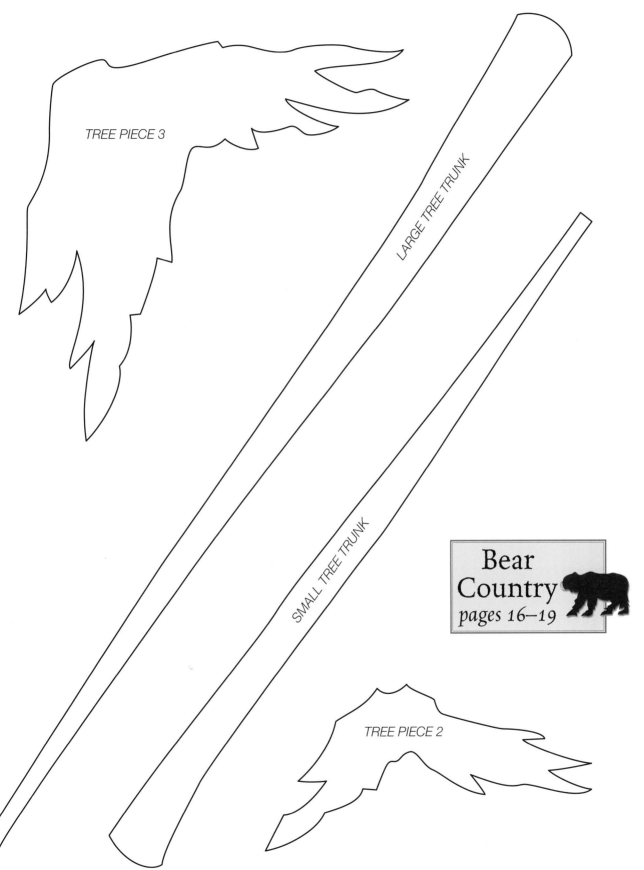

TREE PIECE 3

LARGE TREE TRUNK

SMALL TREE TRUNK

Bear
Country
pages 16–19

TREE PIECE 2

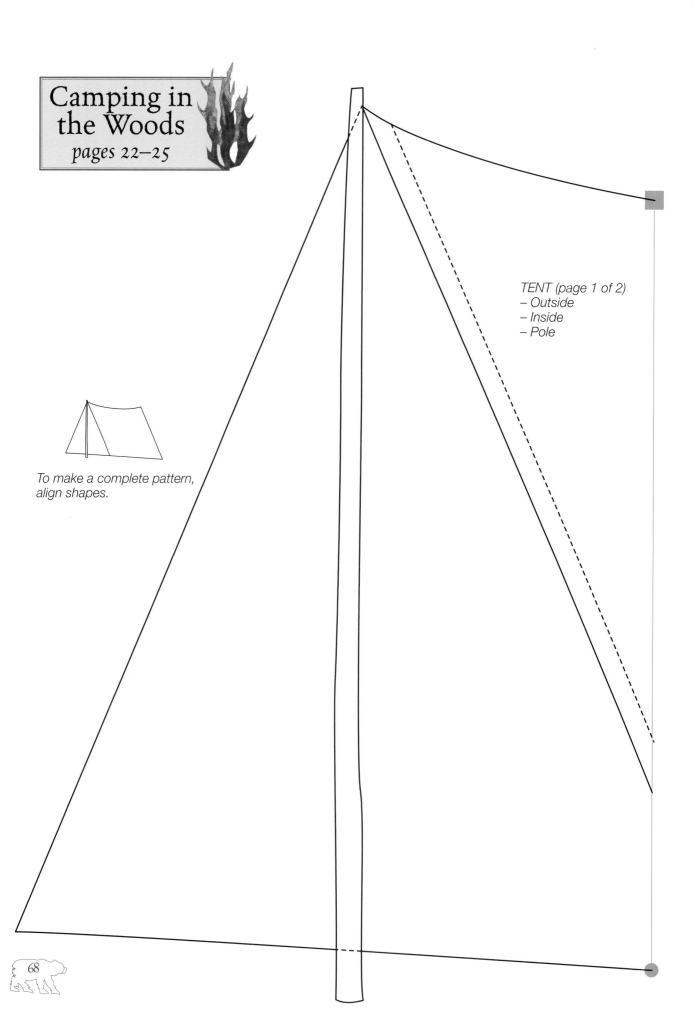

TENT (page 1 of 2)
– Outside
– Inside
– Pole

*To make a complete pattern,
align shapes.*

TENT (page 2 of 2)

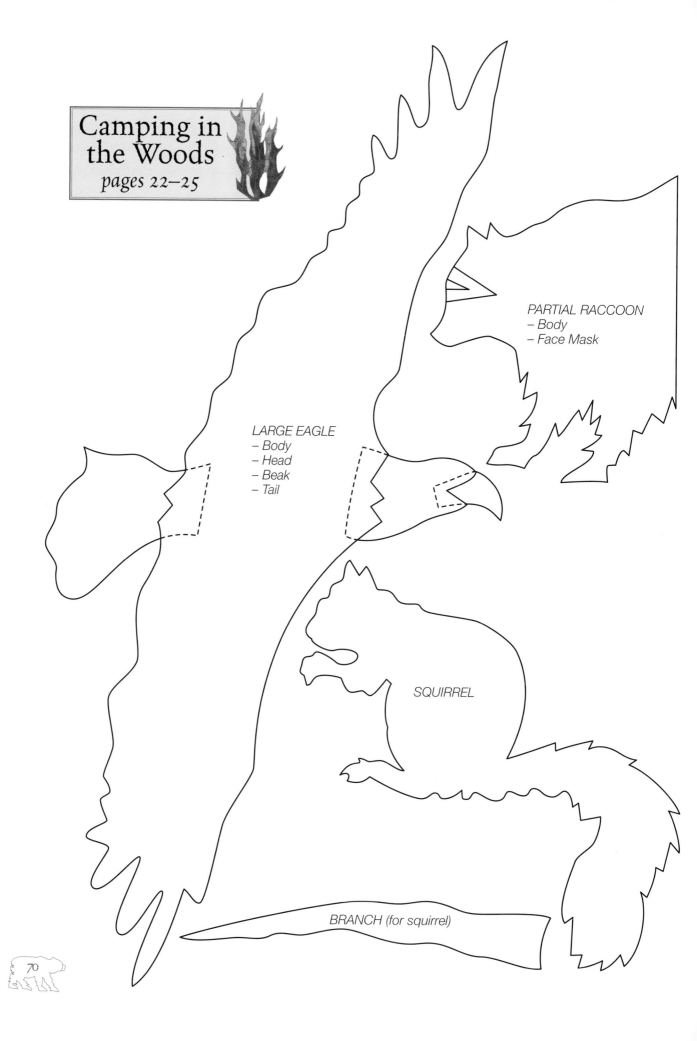

PARTIAL RACCOON
– Body
– Face Mask

LARGE EAGLE
– Body
– Head
– Beak
– Tail

SQUIRREL

BRANCH (for squirrel)

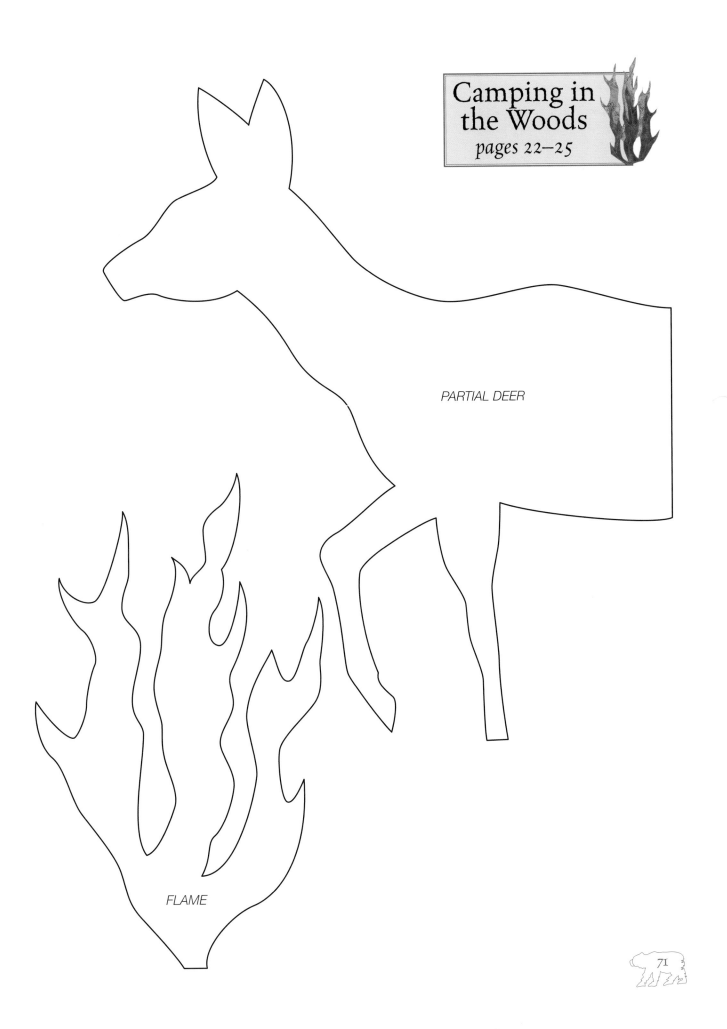

PARTIAL DEER

FLAME

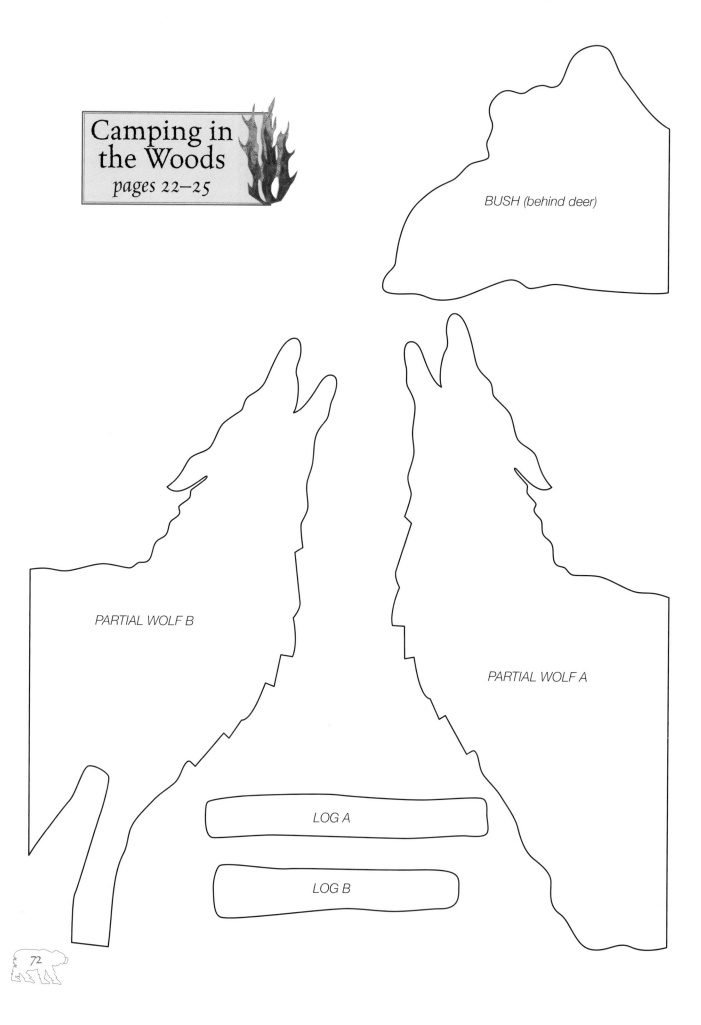

Camping in the Woods
pages 22–25

BUSH (behind deer)

PARTIAL WOLF B

PARTIAL WOLF A

LOG A

LOG B

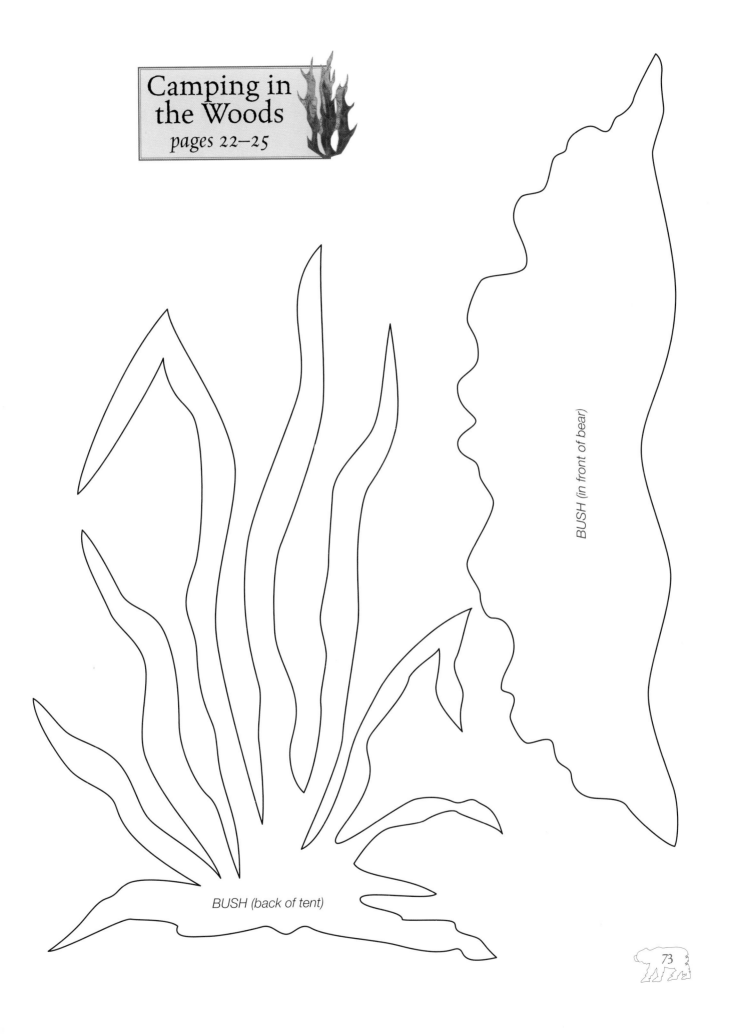

Camping in the Woods

pages 22–25

BUSH (in front of bear)

BUSH (back of tent)

Camping in the Woods

pages 22–25

FIRE PIT ROCK B

BUSH (between bear and moose)

PARTIAL MOOSE ANTLERS

FIREPIT ROCK A

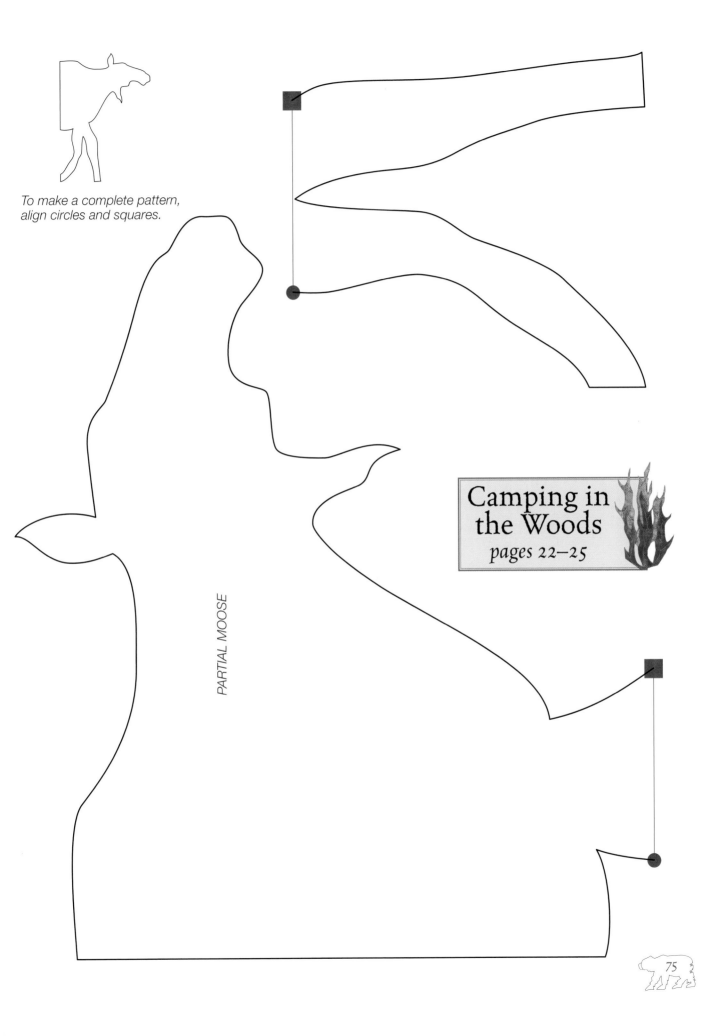

To make a complete pattern,
align circles and squares.

PARTIAL MOOSE

Camping in
the Woods
pages 22–25

75

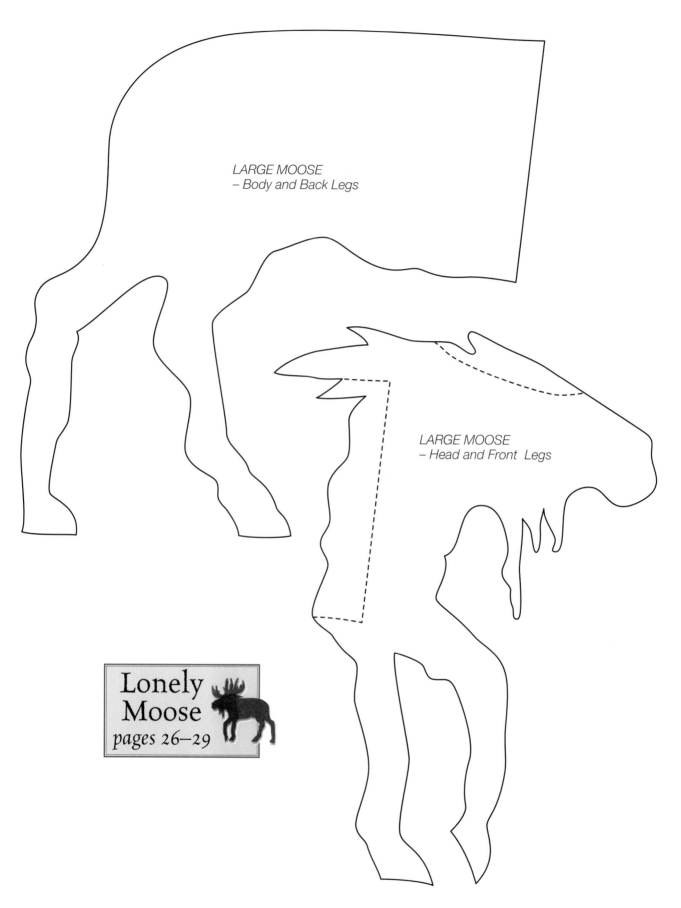

LARGE MOOSE
– Body and Back Legs

LARGE MOOSE
– Head and Front Legs

Lonely
Moose
pages 26–29

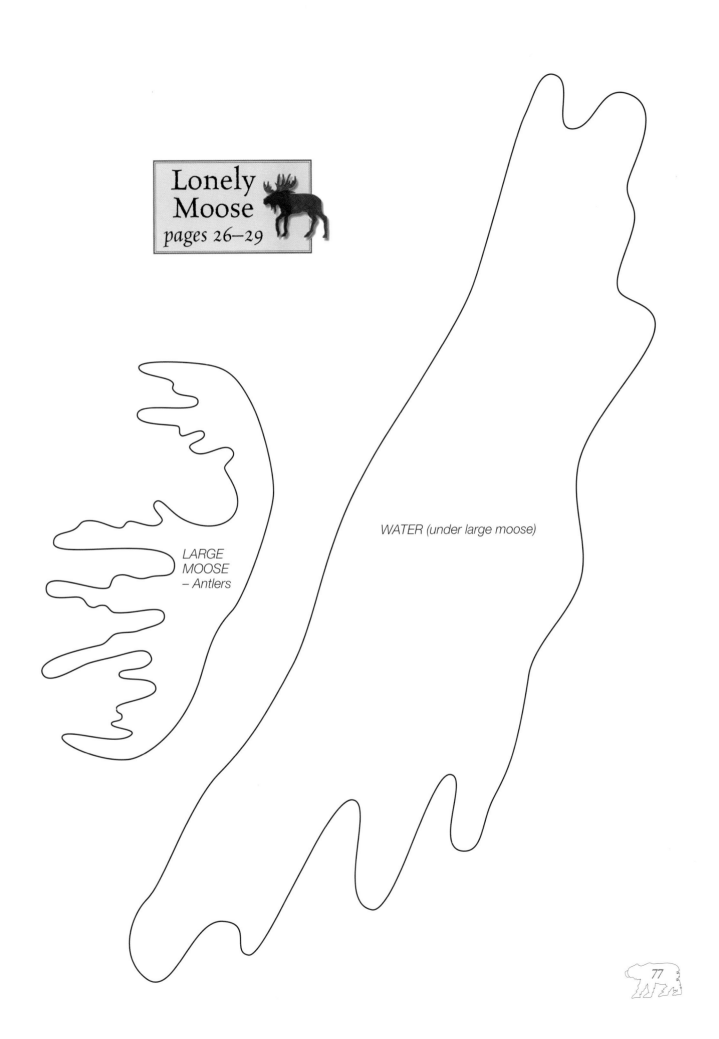

Lonely
Moose
pages 26–29

LARGE
MOOSE
– Antlers

WATER (under large moose)

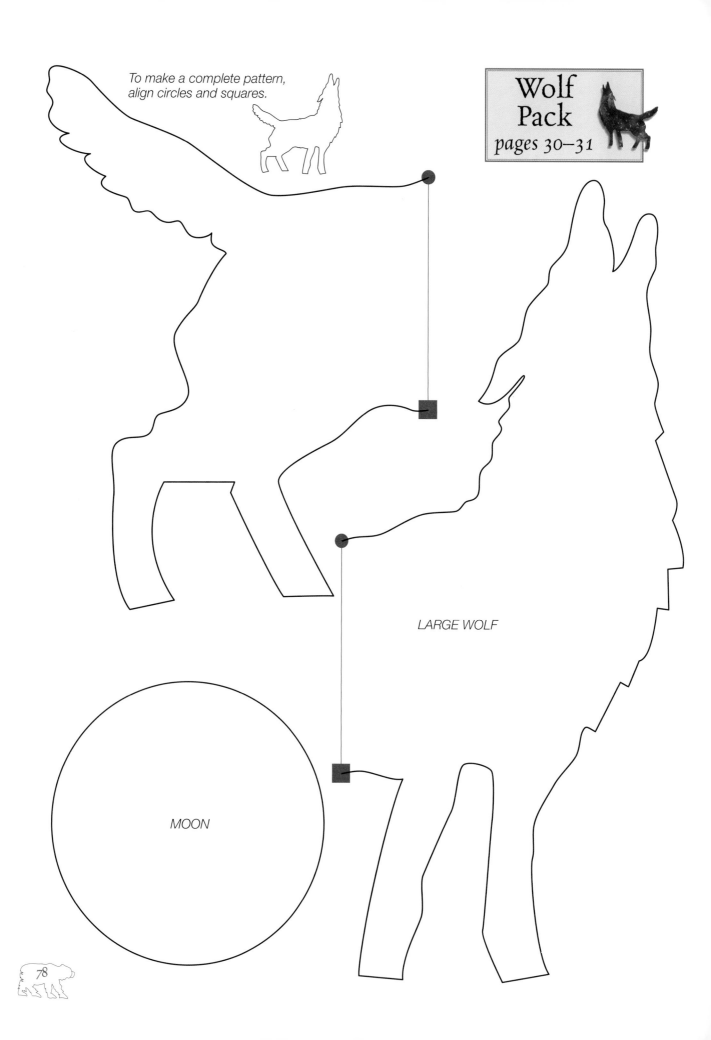

To make a complete pattern, align circles and squares.

Wolf Pack
pages 30–31

LARGE WOLF

MOON

78

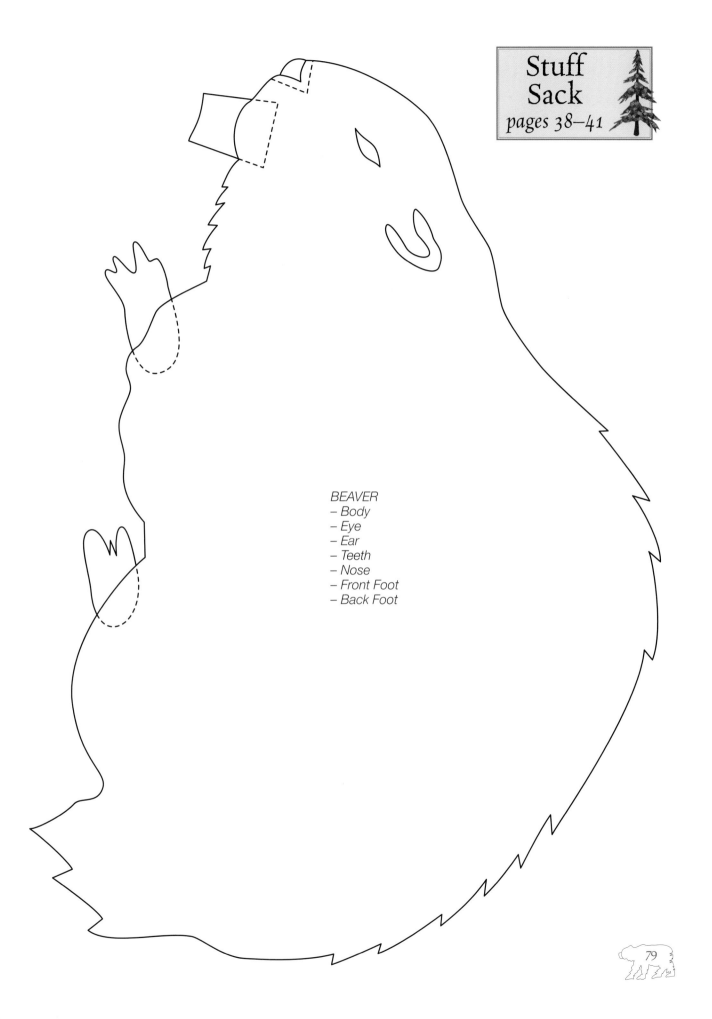

BEAVER
– Body
– Eye
– Ear
– Teeth
– Nose
– Front Foot
– Back Foot

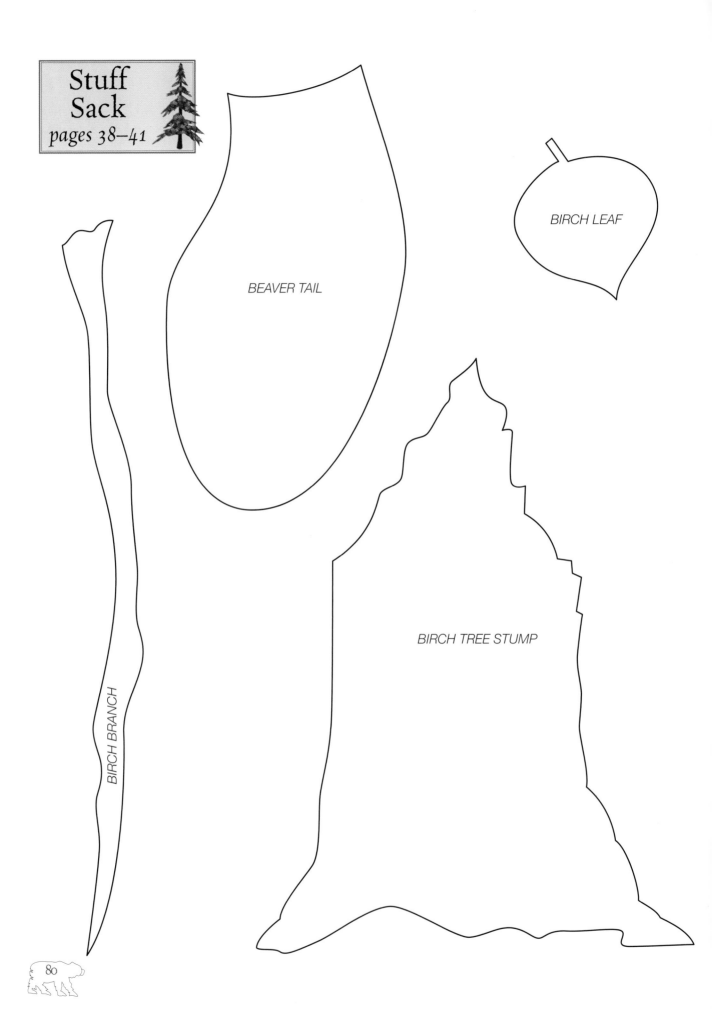

Stuff
Sack
pages 38–41

BIRCH LEAF

BEAVER TAIL

BIRCH TREE STUMP

BIRCH BRANCH

80

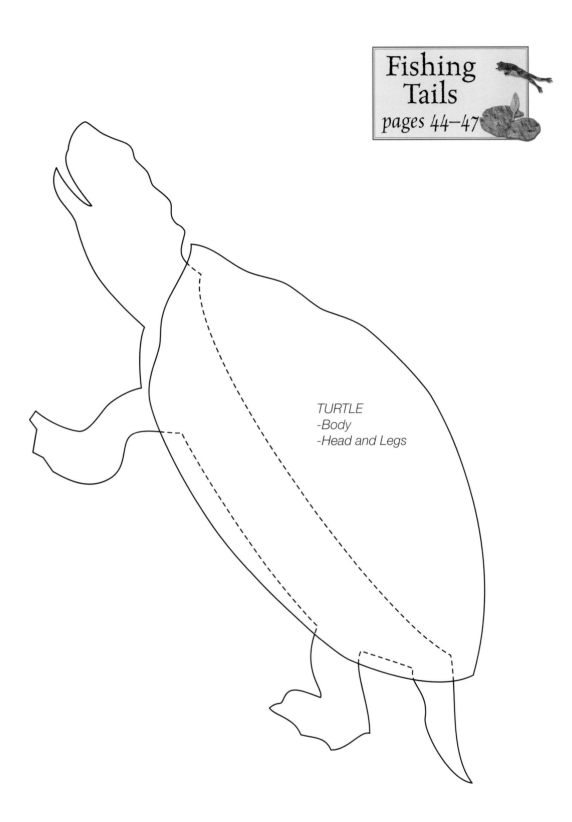

TURTLE
-Body
-Head and Legs

FISHING TALES SCENE (page 1 of 2)
– Fishing Pole
– Father Hair
– Father Face and Hands
– Father Shirt and Arm
– Father Slacks
– Son Hair
– Son Face and Hand
– Son Shirt
– Boat Trim
– Boat
– Water and Water Reflection

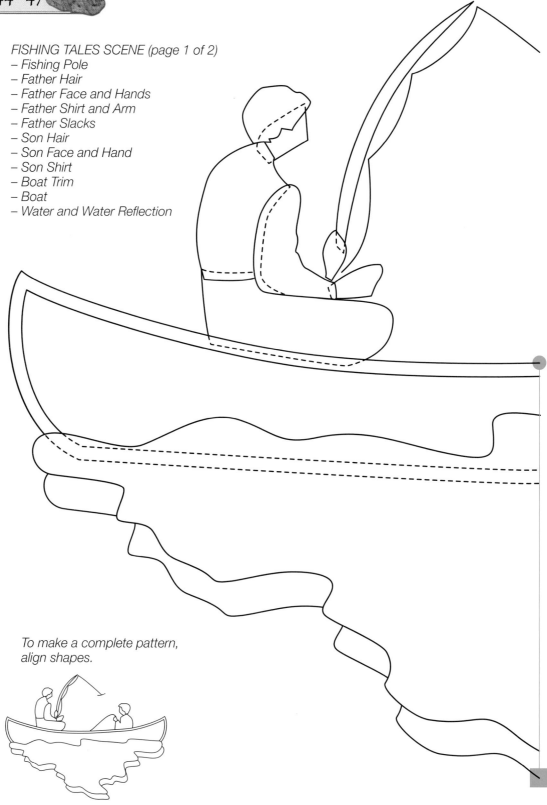

To make a complete pattern,
align shapes.

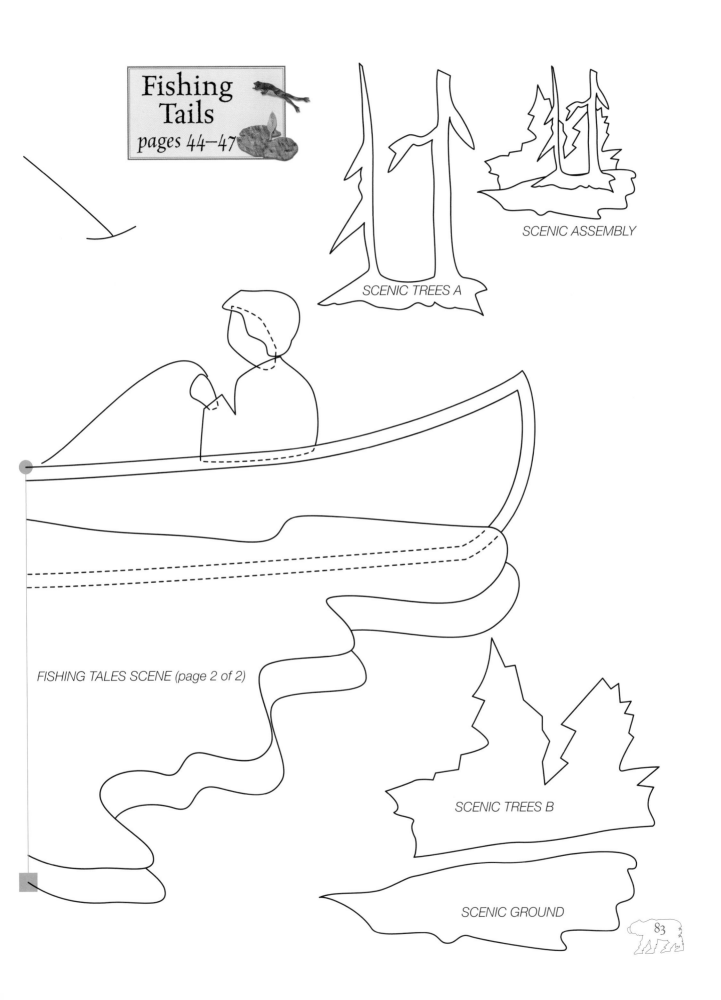

Fishing
Tails
pages 44–47

SCENIC ASSEMBLY

SCENIC TREES A

FISHING TALES SCENE (page 2 of 2)

SCENIC TREES B

SCENIC GROUND

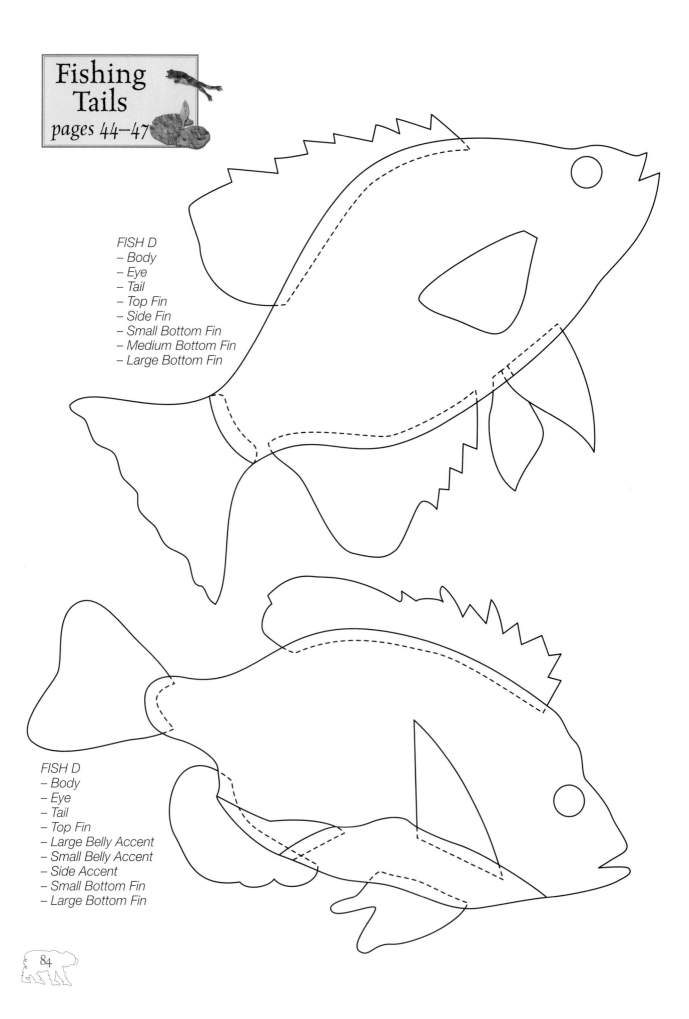

Fishing Tails
pages 44–47

FISH D
– Body
– Eye
– Tail
– Top Fin
– Side Fin
– Small Bottom Fin
– Medium Bottom Fin
– Large Bottom Fin

FISH D
– Body
– Eye
– Tail
– Top Fin
– Large Belly Accent
– Small Belly Accent
– Side Accent
– Small Bottom Fin
– Large Bottom Fin

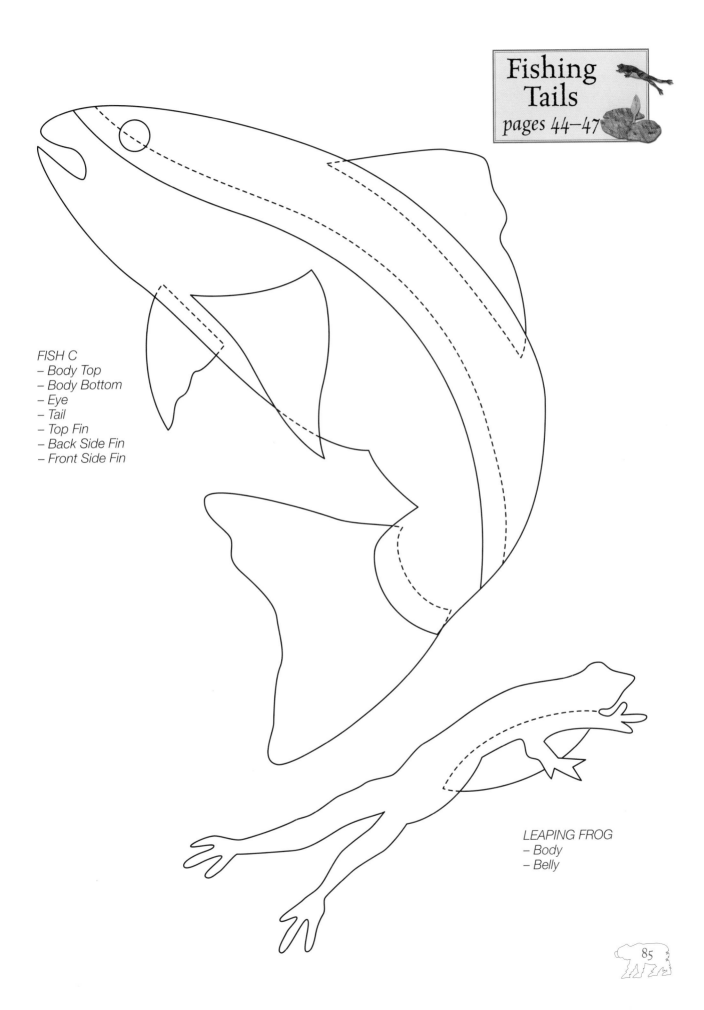

FISH C
– Body Top
– Body Bottom
– Eye
– Tail
– Top Fin
– Back Side Fin
– Front Side Fin

LEAPING FROG
– Body
– Belly

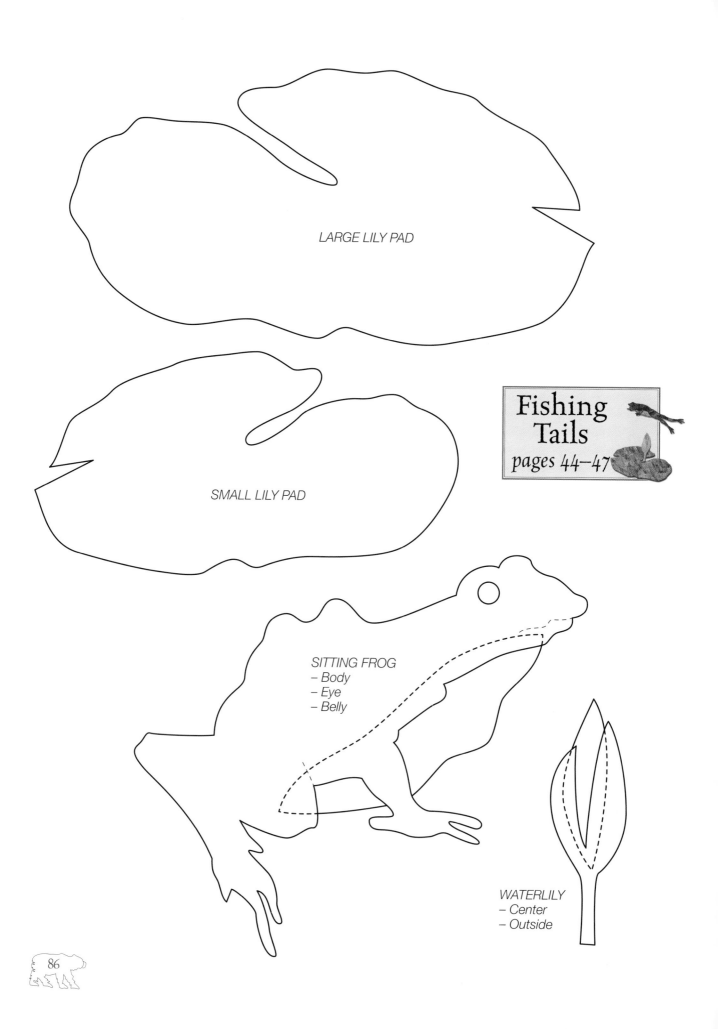

LARGE LILY PAD

SMALL LILY PAD

Fishing Tails
pages 44–47

SITTING FROG
– Body
– Eye
– Belly

WATERLILY
– Center
– Outside

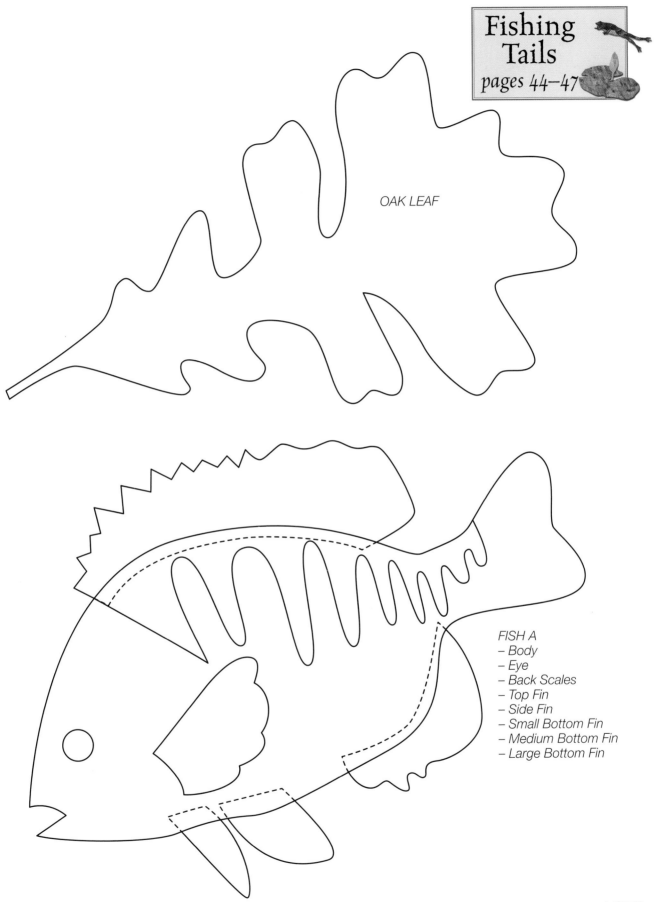

OAK LEAF

FISH A
– Body
– Eye
– Back Scales
– Top Fin
– Side Fin
– Small Bottom Fin
– Medium Bottom Fin
– Large Bottom Fin

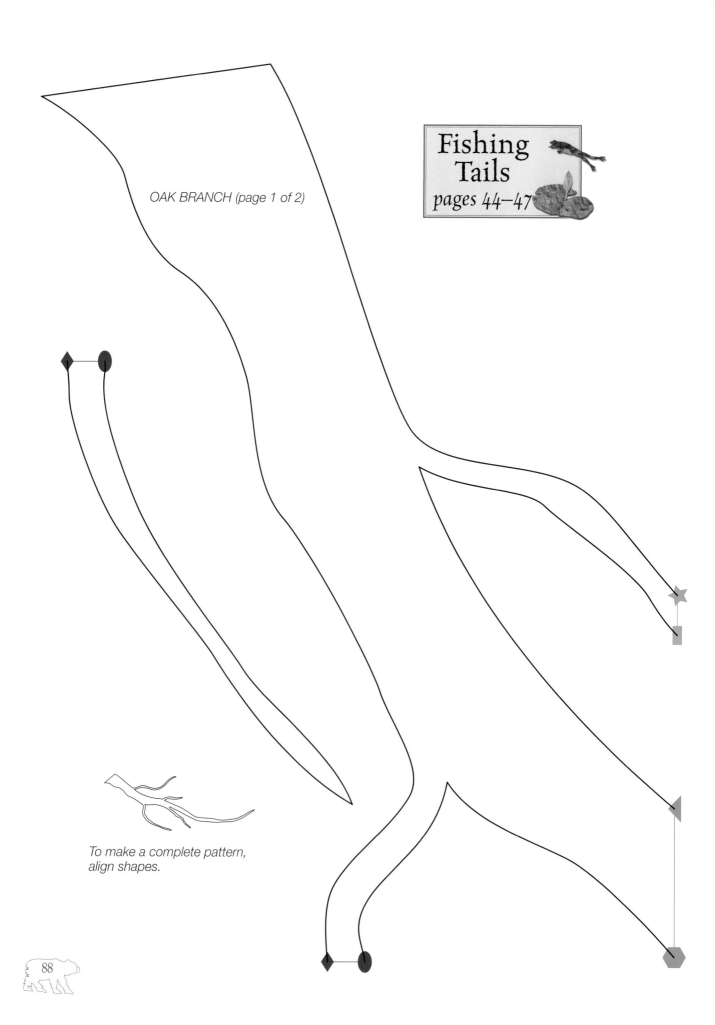

OAK BRANCH (page 1 of 2)

*To make a complete pattern,
align shapes.*

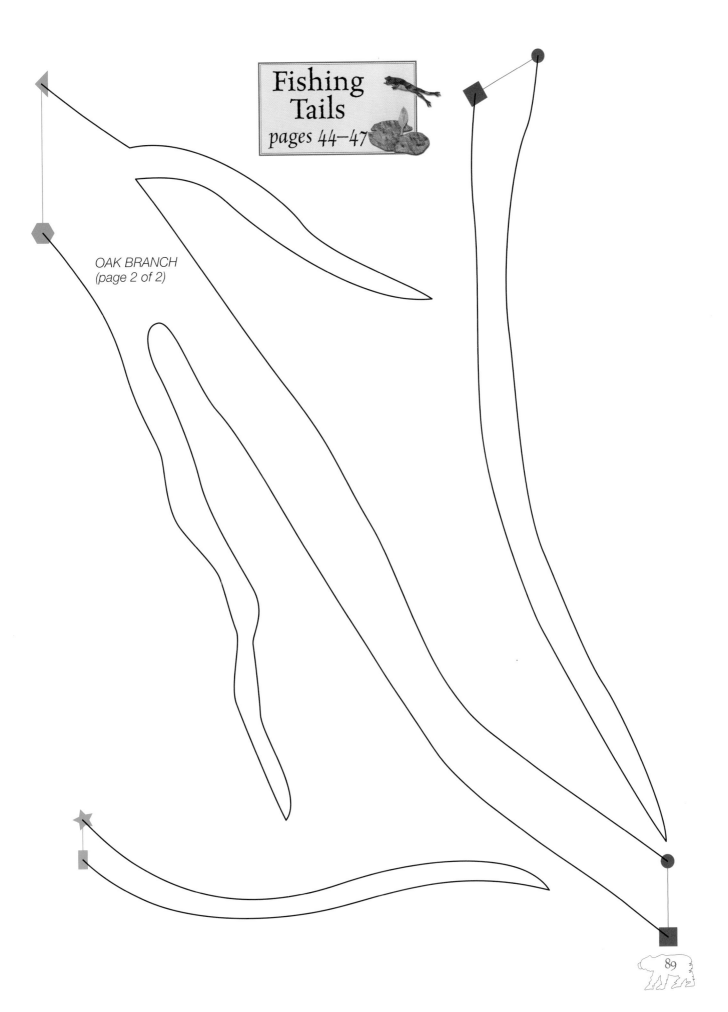

Fishing
Tails
pages 44–47

OAK BRANCH
(page 2 of 2)

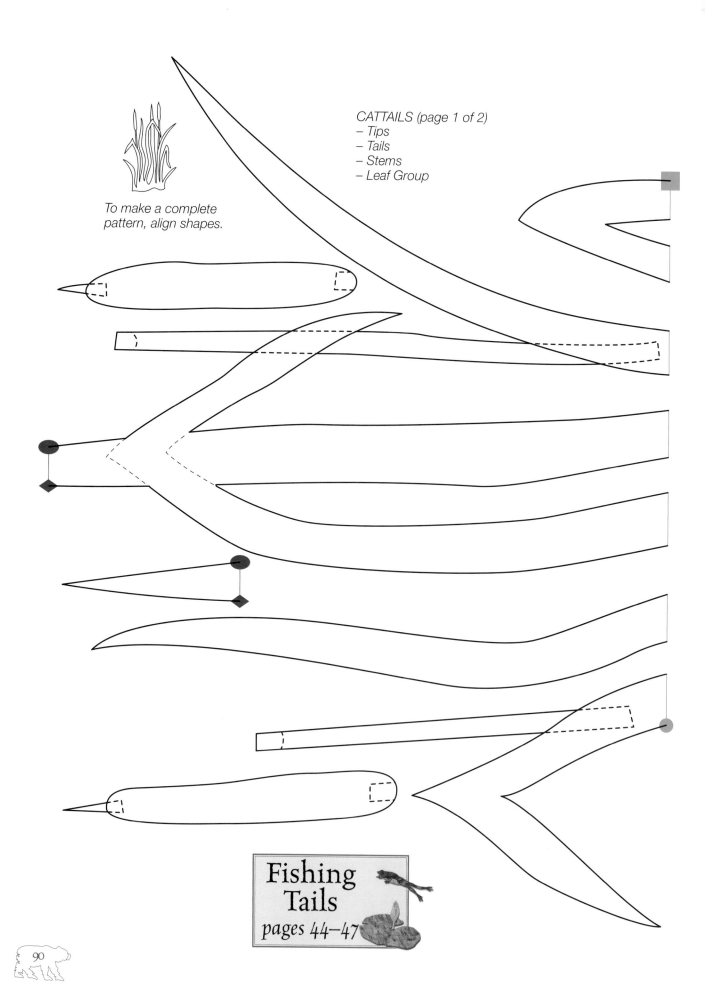

CATTAILS (page 1 of 2)
– Tips
– Tails
– Stems
– Leaf Group

To make a complete
pattern, align shapes.

Fishing
Tails
pages 44–47

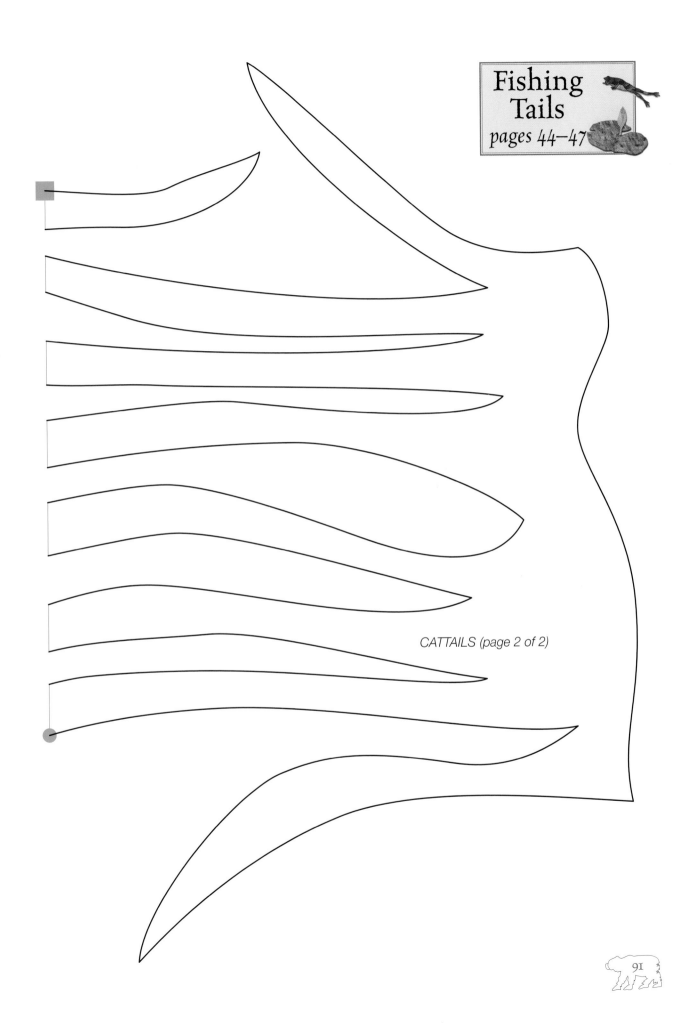

CATTAILS (page 2 of 2)

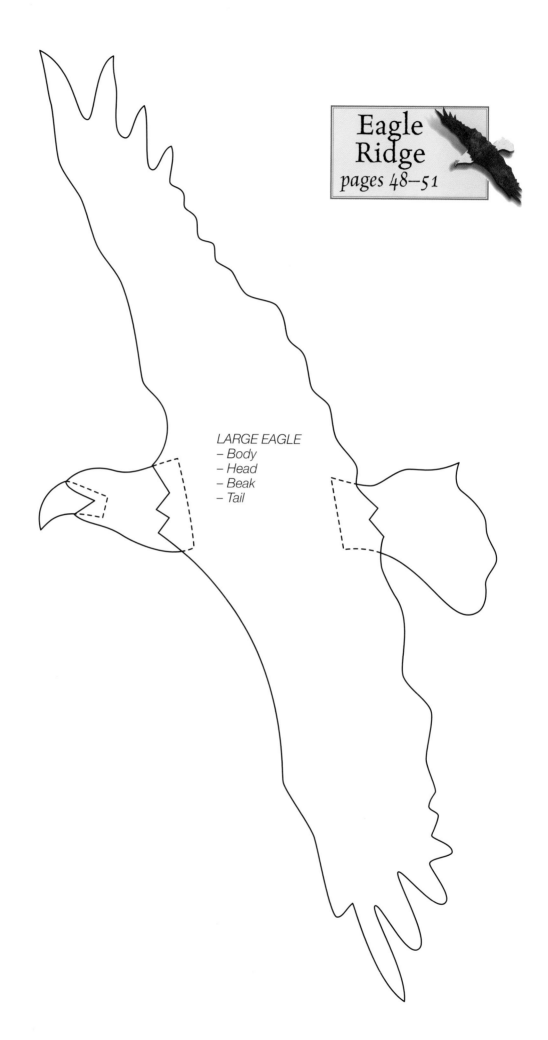

LARGE EAGLE
– Body
– Head
– Beak
– Tail

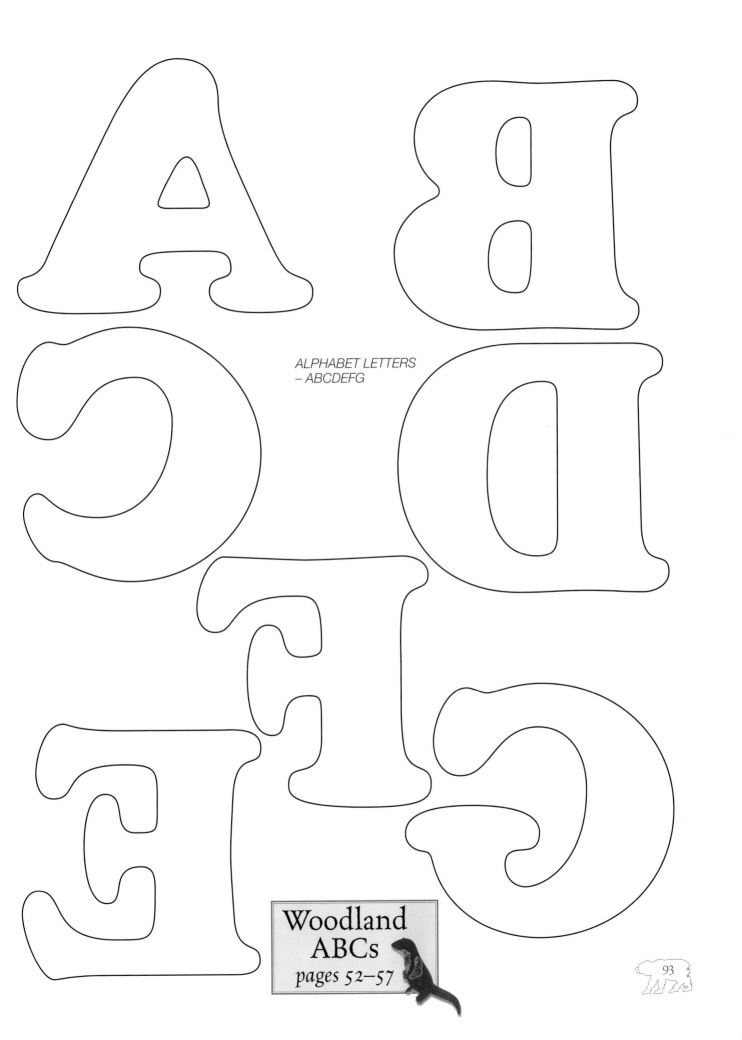

ALPHABET LETTERS
– ABCDEFG

Woodland
ABCs
pages 52–57

93

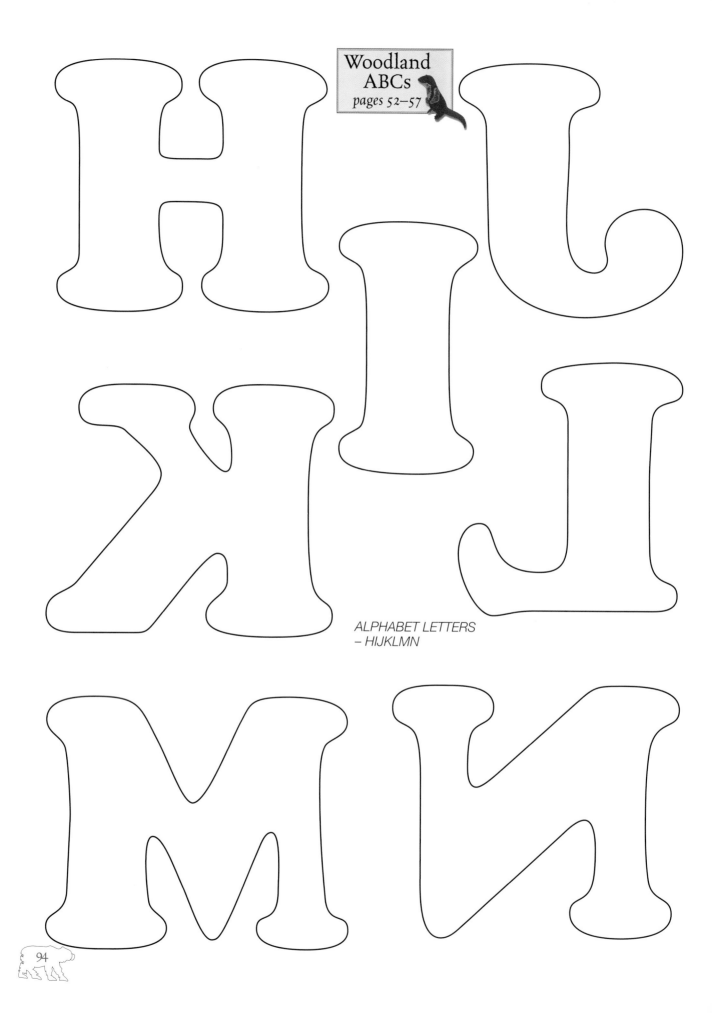

ALPHABET LETTERS
– HIJKLMN

94

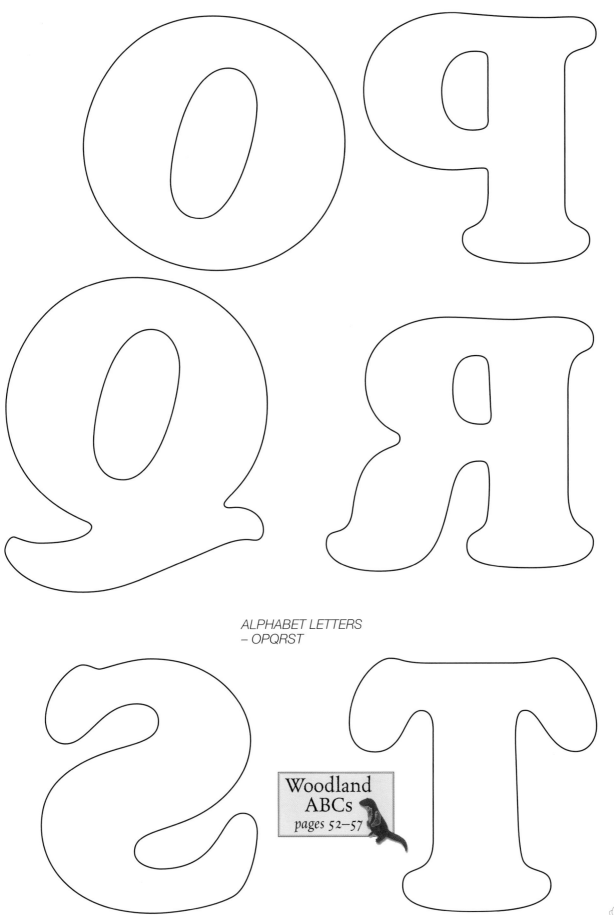

*ALPHABET LETTERS
– OPQRST*

Woodland
ABCs
pages 52–57

Woodland
ABCs
pages 52–57

ALPHABET LETTERS
– UVWXYZ

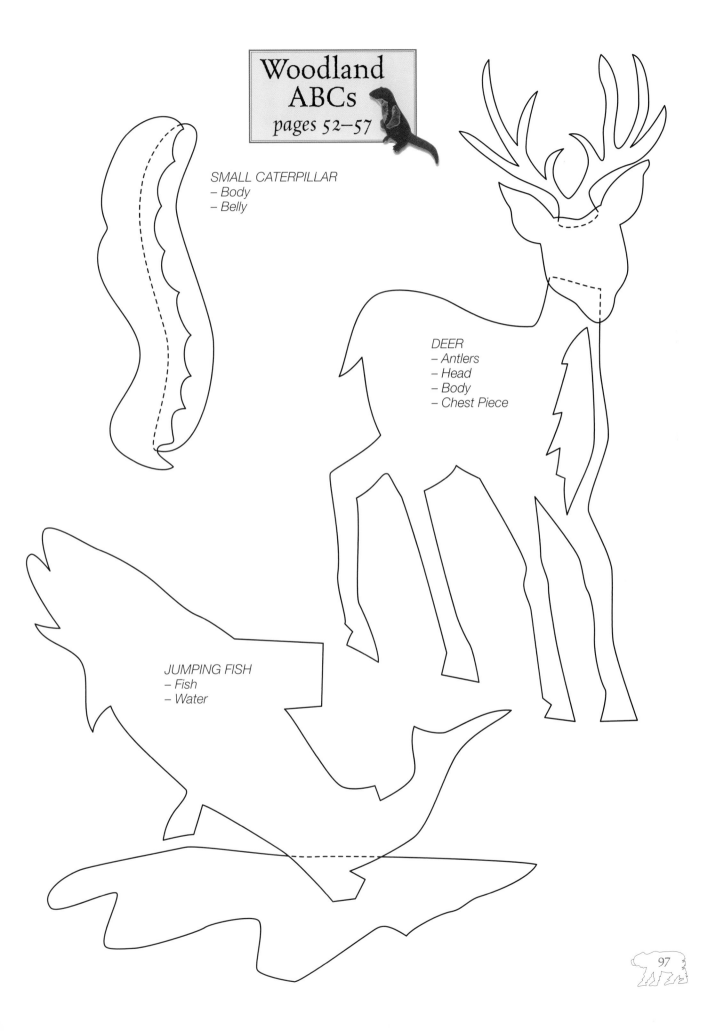

Woodland ABCs
pages 52–57

SMALL CATERPILLAR
– Body
– Belly

DEER
– Antlers
– Head
– Body
– Chest Piece

JUMPING FISH
– Fish
– Water

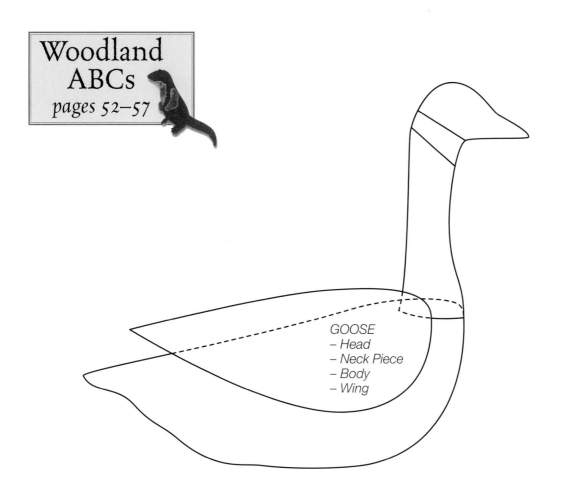

GOOSE
– Head
– Neck Piece
– Body
– Wing

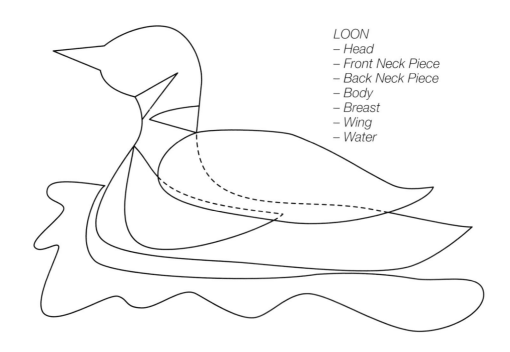

LOON
– Head
– Front Neck Piece
– Back Neck Piece
– Body
– Breast
– Wing
– Water

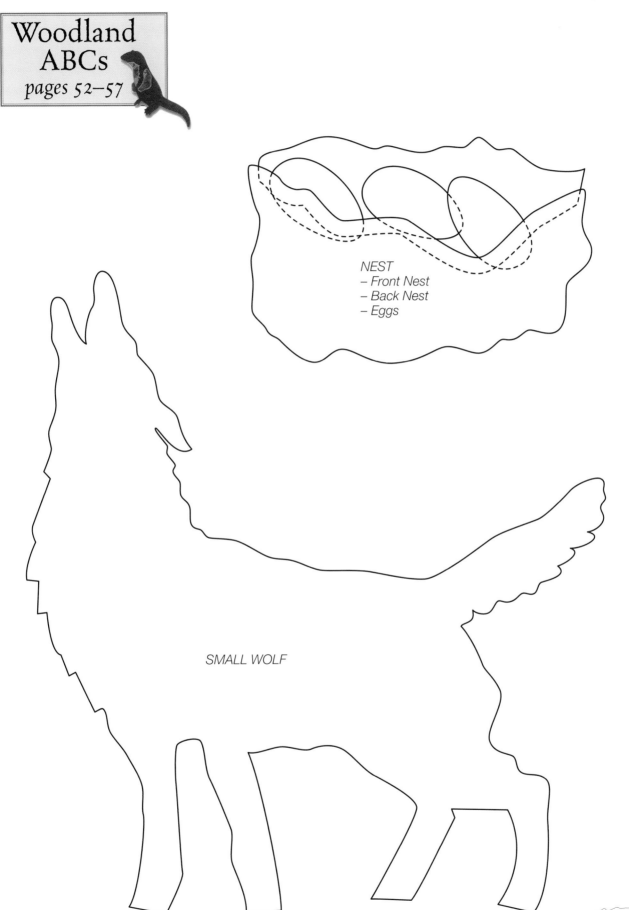

Woodland
ABCs
pages 52–57

NEST
– Front Nest
– Back Nest
– Eggs

SMALL WOLF

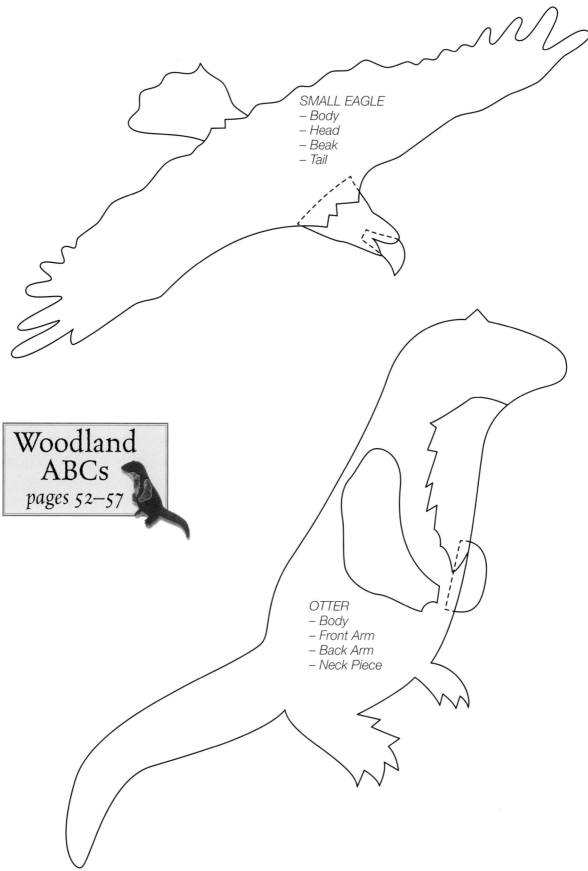

SMALL EAGLE
– Body
– Head
– Beak
– Tail

Woodland
ABCs
pages 52–57

OTTER
– Body
– Front Arm
– Back Arm
– Neck Piece

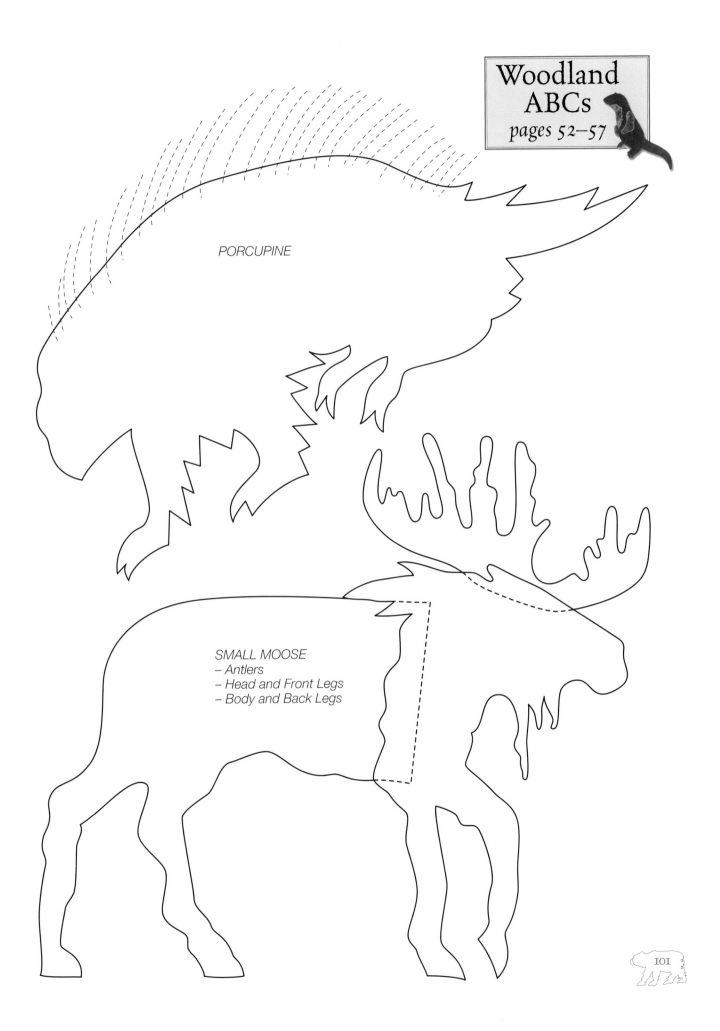

PORCUPINE

SMALL MOOSE
– Antlers
– Head and Front Legs
– Body and Back Legs

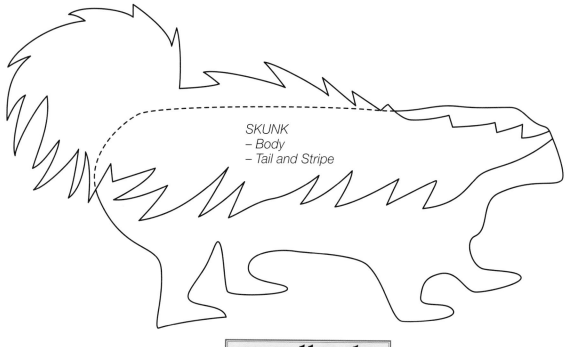

SKUNK
– Body
– Tail and Stripe

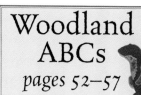

Woodland ABCs
pages 52–57

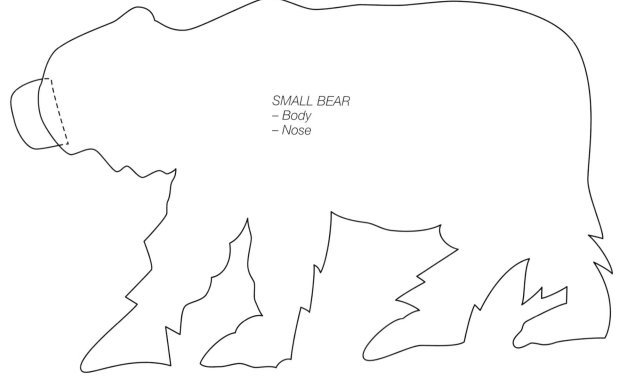

SMALL BEAR
– Body
– Nose

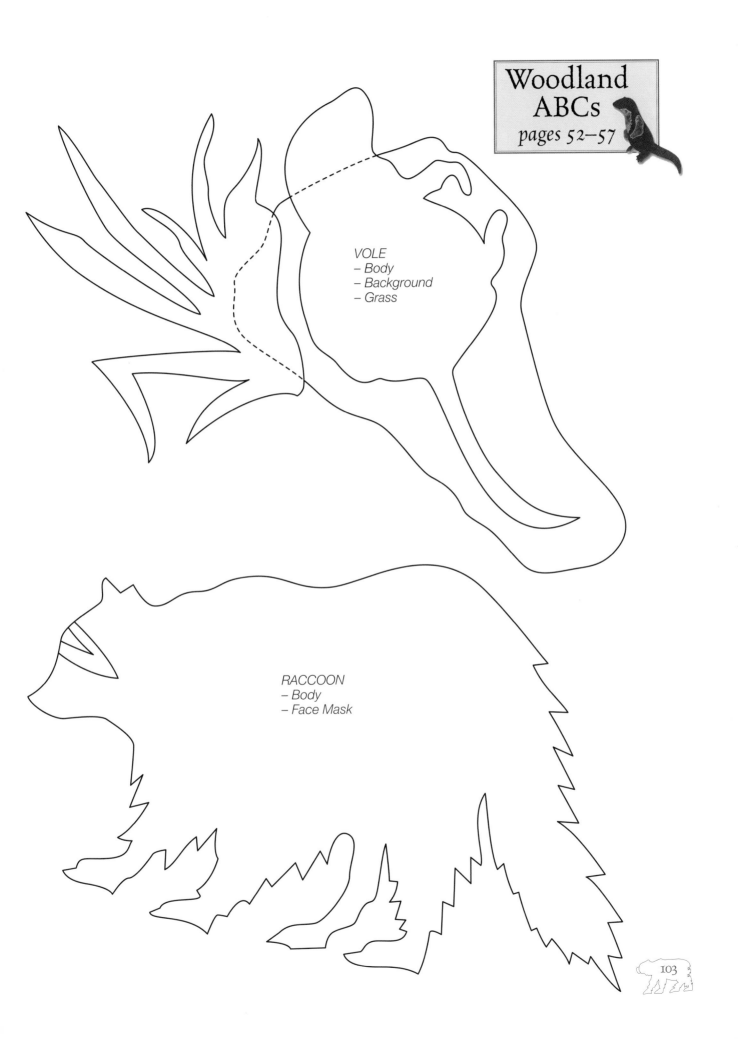

VOLE
– Body
– Background
– Grass

RACCOON
– Body
– Face Mask

LETTERING – DON'T

Don't Bug
Me!
pages 58–61

ANT

LETTERING – BUG ME

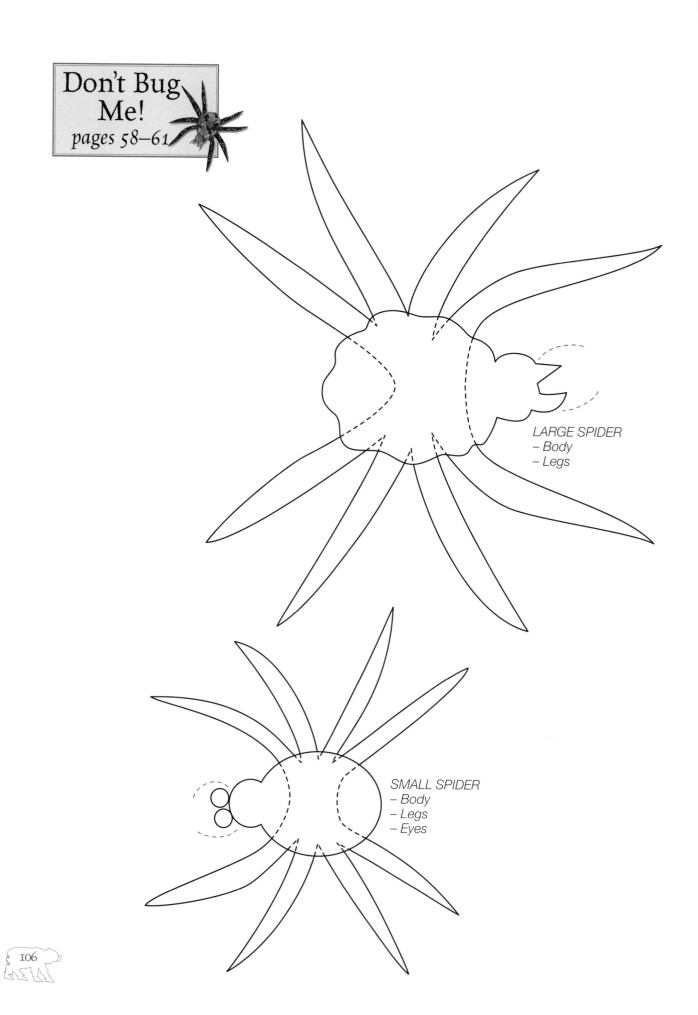

Don't Bug Me!
pages 58–61

LARGE SPIDER
– Body
– Legs

SMALL SPIDER
– Body
– Legs
– Eyes

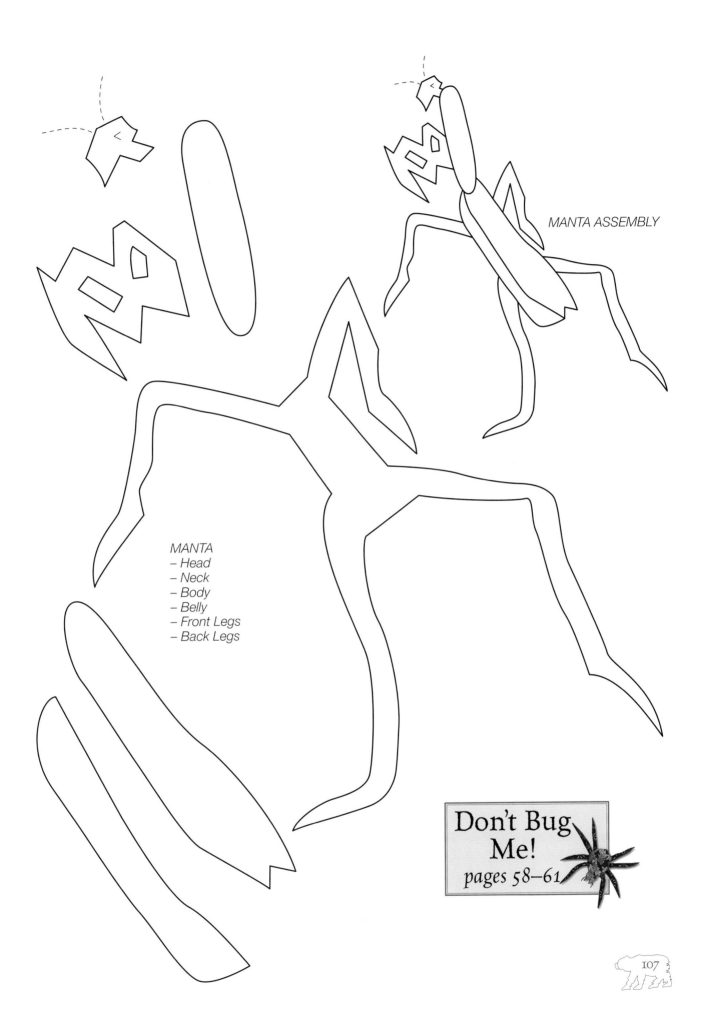

MANTA ASSEMBLY

MANTA
– Head
– Neck
– Body
– Belly
– Front Legs
– Back Legs

Don't Bug Me!
pages 58–61

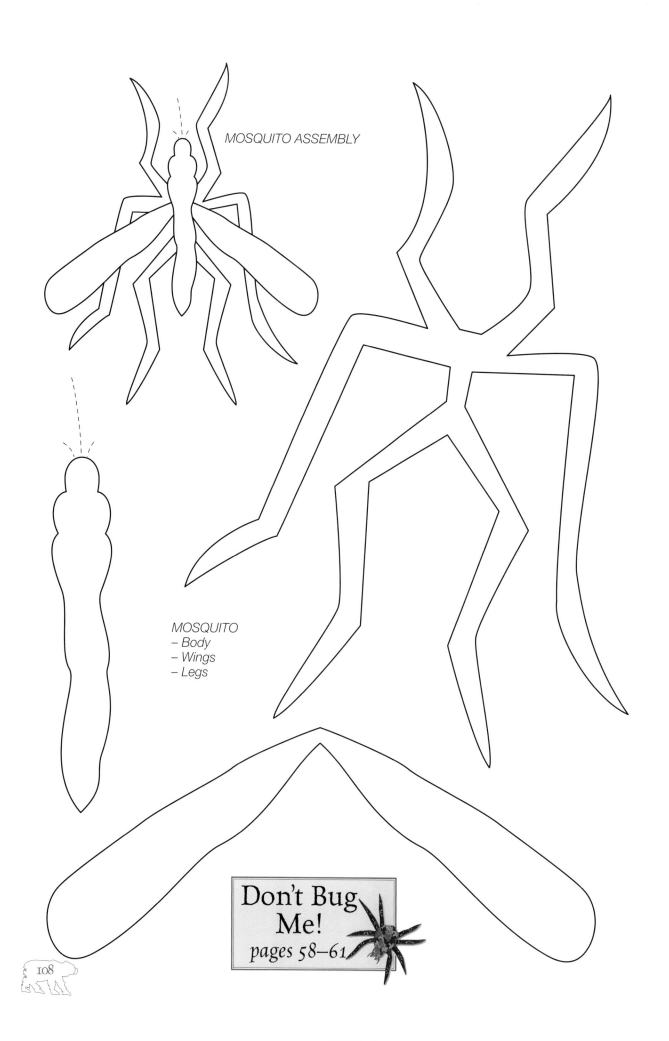

MOSQUITO ASSEMBLY

MOSQUITO
– Body
– Wings
– Legs

Don't Bug
Me!
pages 58–61

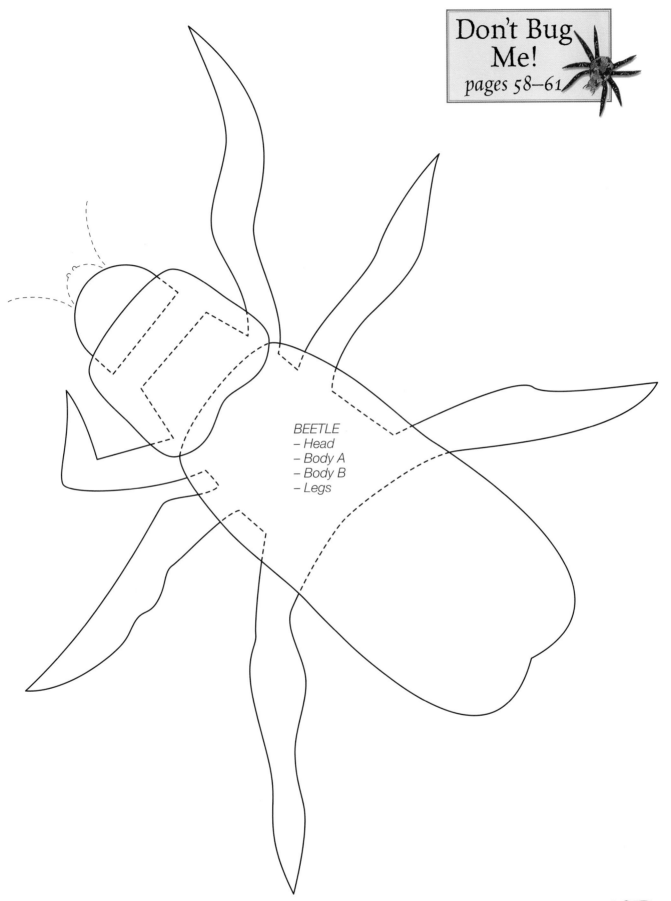

BEETLE
– Head
– Body A
– Body B
– Legs

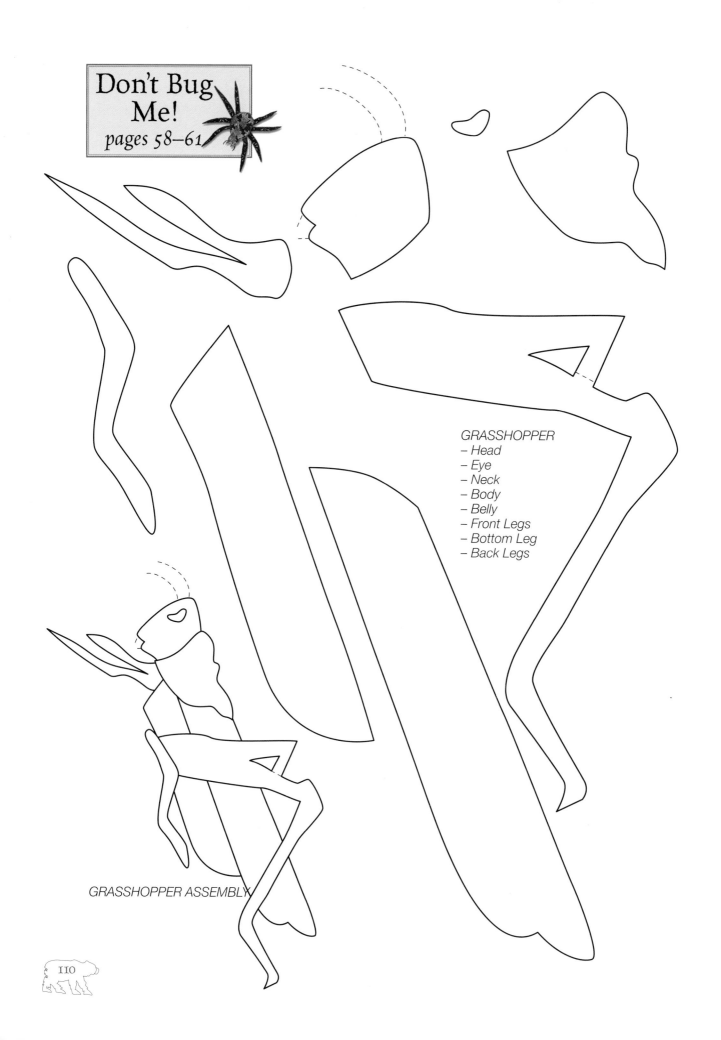

Don't Bug Me!
pages 58–61

GRASSHOPPER
– Head
– Eye
– Neck
– Body
– Belly
– Front Legs
– Bottom Leg
– Back Legs

GRASSHOPPER ASSEMBLY

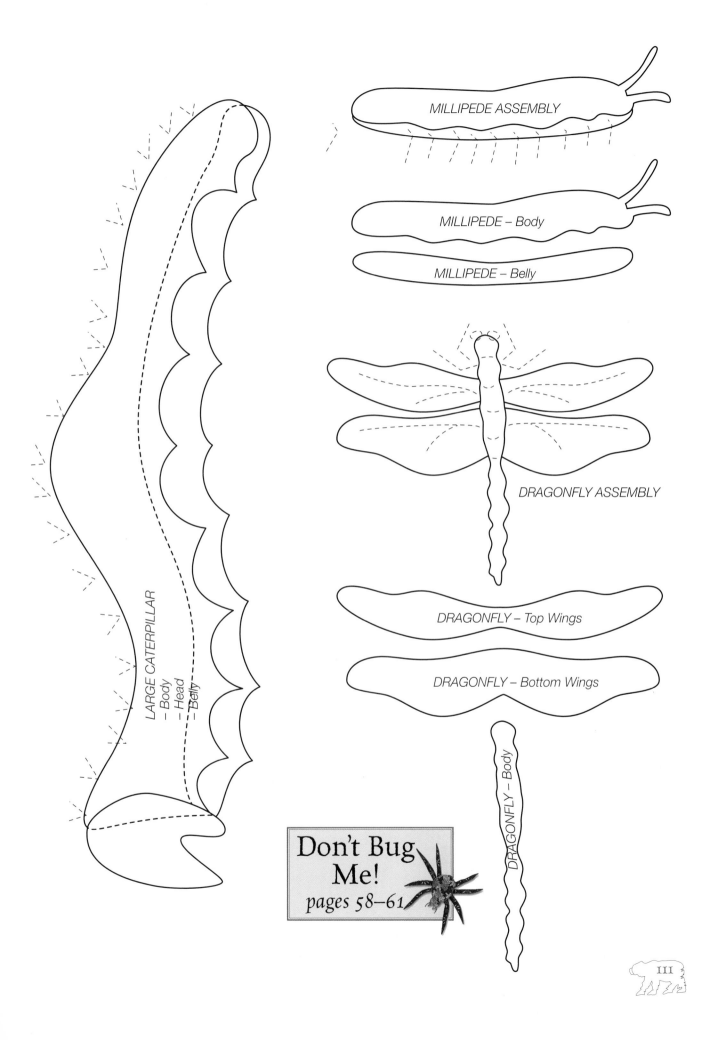

MILLIPEDE ASSEMBLY

MILLIPEDE – Body

MILLIPEDE – Belly

DRAGONFLY ASSEMBLY

DRAGONFLY – Top Wings

DRAGONFLY – Bottom Wings

DRAGONFLY – Body

LARGE CATERPILLAR
– Body
– Head
– Belly

Don't Bug Me!
pages 58–61

III